CONTENTS

POWER REAL ESTATE LETTERS

Third Edition

A PROFESSIONAL'S RESOURCE FOR SUCCESS

William H. Pivar
Corinne E. Pivar

Real Estate Education Company®
a division of Dearborn Financial Publishing, Inc.

This publication is designed to provide accurate and authoritative information in regard to the subject matter covered. It is sold with the understanding that the publisher is not engaged in rendering legal, accounting, or other professional service. If legal advice or other expert assistance is required, the services of a competent professional person should be sought.

Executive Editor: Cynthia A. Zigmund
Managing Editor: Jack Kiburz
Cover Design: Design Alliance, Inc.

Published by Real Estate Education Company,®
a division of Dearborn Financial Publishing, Inc.®

Printed in the United States of America

10   9   8   7   6

Library of Congress Cataloging-in-Publication Data

Pivar, William H.
   Power real estate letters : a professional's resource for success /
   William H. Pivar, Corinne E. Pivar—3rd ed.
   p.   cm.
   Includes index.
   ISBN 0-7931-2474-3
   1. Real estate business—Records and correspondence.   I. Pivar, Corinne E.
   II. Title.
HG1386.5.P58   1994
808'.066333—dc20   96-36008
                                                                             CIP

Real Estate Education Company books are available at special quantity discounts to use as premiums and sales promotions, or for use in corporate training programs. For more information, please call the Special Sales Manager at 800-621-9621, ext. 4384, or write to Dearborn Financial Publishing, Inc., 155 N. Wacker Drive, Chicago, IL 60606-1719.

Chapter 6   Owner Cancellation/Breach of Listing . . 129

Chapter 7   Residential Buyer Solicitation 137

AN INTRODUCTION TO LETTERS

In effective communications, personal contact usually ranks first, and telephone conversations come in second. This leaves letters in third place. Letters do, however, have some distinct advantages over other methods of communication. Besides providing a written record of the communication, which allows little room to question the message conveyed, letters provide a clarity of intent often lost in verbal communication. There are also times when a letter is the only feasible way to communicate effectively because of the recipient's inaccessibility, the sheer volume of people to be contacted or the complexity of the information to be conveyed.

The second edition of *Power Real Estate Letters* puts 279 fresh, persuasive, concise letters at your fingertips. You can easily adapt them to your own audience. These letters enable you to maximize the benefits of writing and sending real estate letters.

Both new and experienced real estate agents need to use their time effectively, and they must establish and maintain relationships with current and future clients. *Power Real Estate Letters* will save you valuable time and effort in creating letters on hundreds of topics. Using these letters will allow you to reach a large number of potential and current clients. Individual agents and entire real estate offices can increase their productivity by using these letter templates.

Which Method Is Best?

This book also provides some letters for situations in which personal contact is often the desired method, such as presenting offers, requesting price reduction or dealing with personnel problems. Consider each situation individually; ask yourself what is your goal and what is the best method of communication for that goal. As long as it is feasible, use the best method, whether that includes letters, personal contact, phone calls or another method.

KISS—Keep It Simple and Sincere

A letter is simply a written message; as such, it must accurately convey what the writer intends to say. In letter writing, the KISS rule applies—*Keep It Simple and Sincere*. In other words, your letter should follow these guidelines:

- Get to the point quickly.

- Use clear and concise language so that readers will not get a message other than what is intended.

- Avoid extraneous material that detracts from or obscures the primary message.

- Be honest.

You may be great at working crossword puzzles because of your extensive vocabulary, but remember that the purpose of your letters is to communicate, not to impress. The most important attribute of any business letter is clarity. It must convey the writer's message to the reader in an unambiguous manner. One of the keys to achieving clarity is brevity. For this reason, the letters in *Power Real Estate Letters* are generally very short and to the point. Short letters are more likely to be fully read and understood by the reader.

Business letters are likely to be read by people who are as jealous of their time as you are of yours. Therefore, the message must be quickly understood. If the reader is not getting the message within the first 15 seconds, chances are that you need to rewrite your letter.

Using Sales Letters as Marketing Tools

Sales letters are different from other business letters. A sales letter is really an ad, which is simply a request for business. Real estate sales letters are intended to sell either your services or property. In advertising, the acronym AIDA is often used. It stands for Attention, Interest, Desire, Action. A sales letter should meet these criteria: it should get the reader's attention, generate interest, create a desire for the product (or for more information) and result in either action by the recipient or an anticipation of your call.

The letter must grab the reader's attention in the first few sentences. Once you have attracted the reader's attention, the entire letter, even an extremely long one, will generally be read. Attention-getting headings can be directed to particular interests of the recipient, or they can even be absurd or humorous statements. The heading must, however, quickly lead to a message of interest; if it doesn't, your solicitation letter will be discarded. Keep in mind that people want benefits and they must be told quickly that benefits are what you are offering them.

In the real estate profession, you should regard the letter as a tool to get you through a door. Letters don't sell property or services—the sale is up to you.

Testing Your Market

All sales letters are not equally successful. Some letters have phenomenal results, while others fail to generate anything other than mailing expense. Because direct mailing is one of the most costly advertising media in terms of the cost for each contact made, you don't want to waste dollars on mailings that fail to maximize results. Your letter copy is important, and we have provided you with various copy choices for listing and buyer solicitations. However, copy effectiveness will vary regionally and among target audiences. We therefore suggest that you test your market using different copy so that you can concentrate on what works most effectively.

To evaluate effectiveness you can use different mailing pieces sent to people whose last names begin with different letters. By knowing the number of pieces mailed and the resulting number of appointments, you will be able to track your percentage of success.

Do's and Don'ts of Soliciting by Mail

Here are some do's and don'ts of soliciting listings or buyers by mail:

Do's:

1. *Your mailing should promise a benefit to the recipient.*

2. *By indicating in the letter that you will call, you more than double the letter's effectiveness.* The reader is forced to give consideration to your message.

3. *Personally address all correspondence.* Never write "To Occupant." Occupants don't buy or sell real estate—real people do.

4. *Address each letter to make it look personal to the recipient.* Handwritten is best, but not always practical. The letter should also be personalized by using the recipient's name. With computer aid, this is a relatively simple task.

5. *Target letters to those likely to be interested in your services.* Use mailing lists or reverse directories that will give you the names of residents from their addresses. This rifle approach is better than a shotgun approach, in which much of the shot misses the mark. For example, if your mailing's goal is to locate buyers for lower-cost housing with low down payments, consider mailing to families within the service area that live in moderately priced rental units.

6. *Include your card in every letter.* If your card has a recent photo of you on it, the card's effectiveness

increases; your reader now identifies your name with a particular person.

Don'ts:

1. *Don't use a postage meter, third class mail, a stick-on address label or a window envelope.* It looks like junk mail and is more likely to be discarded with only a cursory glance.

2. *Don't disguise the purpose of the letter by making your mailing appear to be an official government letter or a check.* Misleading your readers is unethical, and you want to establish yourself as a professional, not a sleazy operator.

3. *Don't use undersized envelopes.* Envelopes that are too small force you to make an awkward fold in the letter.

When you are writing to a person with whom you are acquainted, consider using something like this:

I will be calling you in a few days asking for your help. I would greatly appreciate any referrals you can provide as to your friends and neighbors who might [*need my services / be interested in buying or selling property*].

Most people like to help people they know, so the recipient of the letter will likely give some thought to possible referrals and be receptive when you call.

Testimonials

Testimonials are very effective and can be included as supplements in mailings. If the reader can relate to the person giving the testimonial, by being in similar circumstances or from the same area, the effectiveness of the testimonial increases. To obtain testimonials, all you really have to do is ask. Satisfied buyers and sellers usually respond favorably to such a request. See Chapter 5 to find a sample written request for a testimonial letter.

Lists

You will see that some letters in this book contain lists of items identified by a bullet (•) or a check mark (✓). Lists are very effective in sales letters because the readers's eyes are led naturally down the letter.

Color

Color attracts attention and can be effectively used in flyers and attachments, but the letters should appear personal. Color makes the letter appear to be a mass market piece; this can create a negative impression in selling real estate. A light color such as buff or gray can, however, convey a professional image.

Follow-up Calls

Here are some general tips about making follow-up telephone calls to letter recipients:

1. *Immediately identify yourself* and tie your call to your letter.

2. *Give minimal information.* The more information you give over the telephone, the less your chance will be of obtaining a face-to-face meeting.

3. *Get information—ask questions.* Answering questions with questions is a good technique to use.

4. *Don't ask for an appointment.* Set a time and date to meet the prospective buyers or sellers. You will generally want both parties present when you deal with couples. Use an option of two positive choices, instead of giving readers the option of not meeting with you: "Would you [*and Mrs. Smith*] be available at 4:30 this afternoon, or would 5:00 be more convenient?"

The letters in this book should satisfy more than 90 percent of an average real estate office's letter-writing needs. (Material that is optional or that you can personalize is italicized and placed in brackets to help you customize your letters.) The letters in this book are presented in the block style, just one of several styles that could have been used. (We have left blank lines for the date, recipient's name, address and the signature.) We prefer a pure block style, and others prefer centered dates and signatures. The format is not a significant factor in communication; if you feel more comfortable with another format, please use it.

Have an Idea for a Letter?
Contact Us!

If you think there is a need for letters that are not included in this book, please let us know so we can add them in later editions. You may write us at 75-496 Desert Park Drive, Indian Wells, CA 92210-8356.

Chapter

1

Promoting Yourself: Letting People Know You Are a Real Estate Agent

Letter to Friend or Acquaintance
on Joining Firm

[*Date*]

_____

_____

_____

Dear _____ :

I have recently joined the real estate firm of [*Clyde Realty*] as a [*sales associate*]. After many weeks of study and training, I am now prepared to meet the real estate needs of all my friends and neighbors.

I will be calling you in the next few days to find out if you or any of your friends need any real estate services. I would appreciate any help that you can provide.

Sincerely,

_____

Enclosure: [*Card*]

NOTE: *This letter is written for a new licensee. It will be especially effective if the card includes your picture so the reader can identify your appearance with your letter. Besides your personal friends and neighbors, the letter should go to people you do business with, close friends of family members, parents of your children's friends, members of organizations you belong to, and so on.*

Broker Letter to Neighbors
of New Salesperson

[*Date*]

_____

_____

_____

Dear _____ :

[*Judith Reilly*], your neighbor who lives at [*111 Midvale Lane*], has
recently joined our firm as [*a sales associate / an associate broker*].
[*Judith*] has been your neighbor for [*four*] years. [*She*] and [*her
husband*] have [*two children, Lisa age nine and Jeffrey age seven,
both of whom attend Midvale School.*] [*Judith is a graduate of Ohio
State and previously worked in marketing.*] [*She*] has just completed
our training program and will be specializing in [*residential sales*]
in [*Orchard Ridge*]. If you or any of your friends have any real
estate needs, we hope you will contact [*Judith*]. I have enclosed one
of her new cards.

Sincerely,

_____

Enclosure: [*Card*]

NOTE: *This letter should paint the employee as a person the
reader will want to know. It should be mailed over a radius
of several blocks around the new employee's home as well
as to the employee's special friends and, if the employee
has children, to the parents of his or her children's friends.
The employee's picture should be on the card enclosed so
neighbors who have seen him or her can relate to the
employee.*

Salesperson Letter to Neighbor

[*Date*]

_____

_____

_____

Dear _____ :

I am your [*neighbor / new neighbor*], [*at 3752 Elm Drive—the white house on the corner*].

I am [*a / an*] [*associate broker / real estate salesperson / REALTOR-Associate®*] with [*Clyde Realty*]. I wanted you to know that I am prepared to [*meet any real estate needs that you might have*].

If you or any of your friends have any questions concerning real estate, don't hesitate to call me at [*555-1111*].

Sincerely,

_____

Enclosure: [*Card*]

NOTE: *Add handwritten note, "I will call you in the next few days to discuss any present or future needs you might have." Enclose your card with your photograph. Your card is more likely to be noticed if you attach it to the letter with a paper clip or staple.*

Letter to Friend/Acquaintance
on Designation/Course Completion

[*Date*]

_____

_____

_____

Dear _____ :

[*Just a short note to let you know that I am now entitled to use the professional designation (CRS) after my name. (CRS) stands for Certified Residential Specialist. To achieve this designation, a* REALTOR® *must have met the high standards set by the Residential Sales Council and must have completed a rigorous course of training.*]

[*Just a short note to let you know that I have recently completed a course in (Financial Skills for the Residential Specialist). This course, sponsored by the (Residential Sales Council), has prepared me to (better advise buyers and sellers in matters such as mortgage choice, tax implications and available financial alternatives).*]

I feel that I am now better prepared to professionally help buyers and sellers meet their real estate needs. I will be calling you in a few days to ask for your help. I would appreciate any referrals you can provide of friends of yours who might need professional help in buying or selling real estate.

[*Sincerely, / Your friend,*]

_____

_____

Enclosure: [*Card*]

Letter to Friend, Acquaintance, Past Customer and Client When You Change Offices

[*Date*]

_____

_____

_____

Dear _____ :

Just a note to let you know I am located at a new address. I am now [*a sales associate / an associate broker*] with [*Clyde Realty*] at their office [*on Bellflower Blvd.*]. I really like this office, as we have a group of energetic professionals who work together as a team to meet both buyer and seller needs.

I will be contacting you in the next few days to find out if any of your friends need my real estate services. I would appreciate any help that you can provide.

Sincerely,

_____

Enclosure: [*Card*]

NOTE: *Enclosing a business card that has your photo on it greatly enhances your letter's effectiveness; the reader can then place your face with your name.*

Mail this letter to friends, neighbors, and acquaintances; service people you do business with; members of organizations you belong to (e.g., social, special interest, religious); friends of family members; the parents of your children's friends; previous buyers and sellers you have have dealt with; and your active files of prospective buyers and sellers.

Letter to Friend/Acquaintance, Neighbor, Former Client upon Opening Your Own Office

[*Date*]

_____

_____

_____

Dear _____ :

Guess what! I took the big step! No, [*not marriage / I am already married*]. I have opened my own office (see letterhead). I am now an independent broker [*affiliated with (Century 21)*], [*doing business as* _____].

I am very excited about the move. I can offer [*a full range of investment and residential properties / specialized service for home buyers and sellers in (West Covina).*]

If you are in the area, stop by for coffee and a "Hello"! I will be giving you a call in the next few days to ask for some help. I would greatly appreciate any referrals you can provide of friends and neighbors who might be considering buying or selling real estate in [*West Covina*].

Sincerely,

_____

Enclosure: [*Card*]

NOTE: *Asking for help is an excellent approach to use for a person you are acquainted with. Although letter doesn't mention this, your telephone call should go beyond requesting referrals. You want to handle the reader's own real estate needs as well.*

Offer To Speak

[*Date*]

_____

_____

_____

Dear _____ :

I understand that, like all service organizations, you constantly need speakers. Well, I would like to volunteer.

I have prepared a [*30-minute*] presentation on [*what's happening in Westwood Real Estate Market / how the proposed tax changes will affect our real estate market / why real estate investment makes sense in today's economy*], which I feel will interest most of your members.

I will be calling you in a few days to discuss my proposal.

Yours truly,

_____

Enclosure: [*Card*]

NOTE: *Your chamber of commerce should be able to give you a list of local service organizations and people to contact.*

Chapter

2

Listing Solicitation Letters—General

Warning: It is a violation of federal law to induce people to leave a neighborhood because of fear that values or the quality of life will decline because of changes in the neighborhood of race, sex, ancestry, religion, handicap or familial status regarding new residents.

Some communities have restrictions on the use of listing solicitation letters. While the legality of such restrictions is in doubt, you should, nevertheless, ascertain if your market area has any such restrictions. For specialized mailings, consider the use of mailing lists. Use the yellow pages of your phone book under "Mailing Lists" to find lists available in your business area.

If you are mailing a listing solicitation letter to someone who may have already listed his or her home, we recommend adding the following statement to the end of the letter: "If you have already listed your home for sale with your broker, please disregard this letter."

Buyer/Seller Referral

[*Date*]

_____

_____

_____

Dear _____ :

Our mutual friend, [*Mary Hopkins*], suggested that I contact you. As you may know, I [*found a new home for Mary / successfully helped Mary sell her home*].

I will be calling you in the next few days to arrange a meeting with you to discuss [*your real estate needs / the marketing of your home*]. [*I can even provide you with a free comparative market analysis.*]

Yours truly,

_____

Enclosure: [*Card*]

NOTE: *You could enclose the Free Market Analysis Certificate on page 24 with this letter.*

Want To Know the Value #1

[*Date*]

_____
_____
_____

Dear _____ :

Did you know that

Rumpelstiltskin

could turn straw into gold? We have achieved the same performance with real estate.

Let me show you what a sale of your property could mean in terms of actual cash in your hands. I will be calling you within the next few days to discuss how we can determine the amount of cash that is trapped within your home.

Yours truly,

_____

Enclosure: [*Card*], [*Free Market Analysis Certificate*]

NOTE: *This type of letter can be used for cold canvassing, but it would be especially strong if mailed to people who have financial difficulties because of liens, bankruptcy proceedings, foreclosure, divorce, death in the family, criminal action or automobile repossession.*

You might consider enclosing the Free Market Analysis Certificate (see page 24) with this letter.

If you are mailing a listing solicitation letter to someone who may have already listed his or her home, we recommend adding the following statement to the end of the letter: "If you have already listed your home for sale with your broker, please disregard this letter."

Want To Know the Value #2

[Date]

_____

_____

_____

Dear _____ :

How Much Money Is Locked Up in Your Home?

Because of high demand in *[Orchard Ridge]*, your home has experienced exceptional appreciation. If you wish to explore the possibility of taking advantage of market opportunities, we can supply you with a supported estimate of your home's present market value without *any* cost or obligation on your part.

I will be calling you in about a week to determine if you are interested in knowing what you could receive from a sale of your home.

Yours truly,

_____

Enclosure: *[Card]*

NOTE: *See note to previous letter.*

Only [*Seven*] Days To Sell

[*Date*]

_____

_____

_____

Dear _____ :

It took

Only [*Seven*] Days To Sell!

That's right, it took just [*seven*] days for [*Clyde Realty*] to sell the home of the [*Clarence Jones family*] at [*2738 West Wilson*]. [*We hope you will welcome your new neighbors Henry and Jean Watson. They have two children, Lisa, nine, and Henry, Jr., six.*]

I will be calling you in the next few days to offer you a computer-generated comparative market analysis that shows you what your home would bring in today's market. We supply this service without any cost or obligation in the hope that when you consider selling, you'll think of [*Clyde Realty*].

Yours truly,

_____

Enclosure: [*Card*]

NOTE: *This mailing should be restricted to the area of a recent neighborhood sale. By providing information that is likely to be of interest and asking the recipient to welcome a new neighbor, you increase the likelihood of a positive reception to your call. Be certain you have the seller and owner's permission to send out this letter. You could enclose the Free Market Analysis Certificate on page 24 with this letter. If you are mailing a listing solicitation letter to someone who may have already listed his or her home, we recommend adding the following statement to the end of the letter: "If you have already listed your home for sale with your broker, please disregard this letter."*

We're Sold Out!

[*Date*]

_____
_____
_____ .

Dear _____ :

I'm sorry but

We're Sold Out!

We don't have a home to sell in [*name of subdivision*]. It is simply a case of demand exceeding the supply.

If you are at all contemplating selling your home, consider acting now to take advantage of the favorable market. I will call you in the next few days to offer you a computer-generated comparative market analysis without any cost or obligation whatsoever, a service of [*Clyde Realty*].

Yours truly,

_____

Enclosure: [*Card*]

NOTE: *You could enclose the Free Market Analysis Certificate on page 24 with this letter. If you are mailing a listing solicitation letter to someone who may have already listed his or her home, we recommend adding the following statement to the end of the letter: "If you have already listed your home for sale with your broker, please disregard this letter."*

I Apologize

[*Date*]

_____

_____

_____

Dear _____ :

I Apologize

If you want to buy a home in [*Claridge Estates*], I don't really have much to show you. There has been a terrific demand, and the few owners who have taken advantage of the market quickly sold their homes. However, if you really want to buy, call me and I will put your name on my list of buyers.

Now if you are interested in selling, that's a different story! I can prepare for you a computer printout of recent comparable sales, indicating the price range we can anticipate from a sale in the current market. This service is at *no* cost or obligation to you. Because the market is affected by economic change, a future sale could possibly benefit you far less than is possible now.

I will be calling you in the next few days to determine if you want to take advantage of my free offer.

Yours truly,

_____

Enclosure: [*Card*]

NOTE: *You could enclose the Free Market Analysis Certificate on page 24 with this letter. If you are mailing a listing solicitation letter to someone who may have already listed his or her home, we recommend adding the following statement to the end of the letter: "If you have already listed your home for sale with your broker, please disregard this letter."*

Sorry I Missed You

Sorry I Missed You!

I was checking your neighborhood for real estate needs. If you would like to know the present value of your home, I can provide you with a computer-generated comparative market analysis that indicates what you could expect to sell your home for in our present market. We provide this service at absolutely no cost or obligation.

Call Me Now

....

Clarence Beyer
Sales Associate
Clyde Realty   [*555-8200*]

              Evenings: [*555-6173*]

- -

[Photo Business Card]

NOTE: *This is a door hanger to be left on the front door when no one answers. By perforating the door hanger, the business card can be detached.*

Birth of Son or Daughter
(Condominium or Mobile Home Owner)

[*Date*]

_____

_____

_____

Dear _____ :

Congratulations on the birth of your [*son, John / daughter, Mary-Jane*]! It won't be long before [*he / she*] will be running around in seemingly perpetual motion. You will probably be considering purchasing a home with your own backyard for [*John / Mary-Jane*].

I can help you not only find the perfect home but also sell your [*condominium / mobile home*]. Our office provides a computer-generated comparative market analysis that indicates what you could expect to receive on a sale of your [*condominium / mobile home*] in today's market. We provide this service without *any* cost or obligation on your part! We can also analyze your finances and explain current lender requirements and possible loan opportunities.

I will be calling you in the next few days to discuss your housing needs.

Yours truly,

_____

Enclosure: [*Card*]

NOTE: *From the addresses in birth announcements in local newspapers, you can ascertain if the parents live in condominiums or mobile homes. These parents are likely prospects for both a listing and a sale. You could enclose the Free Market Analysis Certificate on page 24 with this letter. If you are mailing a listing solicitation letter to someone who may have already listed his or her home, we recommend adding the following statement to the end of the letter: "If you have already listed your home for sale with your broker, please disregard this letter."*

Graduation of Son or Daughter

[*Date*]

_____

_____

_____

Dear _____ :

Our congratulations! I bet that you feel both proud and glad your [*son / daughter*] has graduated from [*high school / college*]. Now you will probably be able to think about your own needs.

Perhaps you want a smaller home, or the low-maintenance lifestyle of an apartment, condominium or mobile home. Perhaps you want to retire and head for a warmer climate. Whatever your housing needs are, I can help you.

Before you make any decisions, you should know exactly where you stand. I will be happy to furnish you with a [*computer-generated*] comparative market analysis that indicates the present value of your home. In this way, you will know what to expect if you decide to sell. I will be calling you in the next few days to find out if you would like this free analysis, offered without any cost or obligation.

Yours truly,

_____

Enclosure: [*Card*]

NOTE: *This letter is very effective when mailed to single parents. This information may be available from graduation announcements or by cross-checking with specialized mailing lists. You could enclose the Free Market Analysis Certificate on page 24 with this letter. If you are mailing a listing solicitation letter to someone who may have already listed his or her home, we recommend adding the following statement to the end of the letter: "If you have already listed your home for sale with your broker, please disregard this letter."*

Marriage of Son or Daughter

[*Date*]

_____

_____

_____

Dear _____ :

Congratulations! Now that your [*son / daughter*] is married, you probably feel happiness mixed with relief and even sadness. It is, however, a time when you can begin thinking more about your own needs.

Perhaps you want a smaller home, a low-maintenance home or a different lifestyle. You may even be considering retirement. Whatever your housing needs are, I can help you.

Before you make any decisions, you should know your complete financial picture. I'll be happy to prepare a computer-generated comparative market analysis that indicates the present value of your home. In this way, you will know what to expect if you decide to sell.

I will be calling you in the next few days to personally offer you this free analysis without any cost or obligation on your part.

Yours truly,

_____

Enclosure: [*Card*]

NOTE: *This letter is especially effective when sent to single parents. You could enclose the Free Market Analysis Certificate on page 24 with this letter.*

If you are mailing a listing solicitation letter to someone who may have already listed his or her home, we recommend adding the following statement to the end of the letter: "If you have already listed your home for sale with your broker, please disregard this letter."

Retirement

[*Date*]

_____

_____

_____

Dear _____ :

Congratulations on your retirement! I wish you many happy years to enjoy the fruits of your labor.

Many retirees move to areas such as Florida or Arizona for the mild climate, relaxed lifestyle and the common interests of retirement communities, as well as the lower housing costs. Chances are that you could sell your home, buy a nice home or condominium in Florida or Arizona and have cash left over to invest, to supplement your retirement income.

Before you make any decisions, you should first know exactly where you stand. I will be happy to prepare a computer-generated comparative market analysis that indicates the value of your home in the present market. In this way, you will know what to expect if you decide to sell. I will be calling you in the next few days to find out if you would like to obtain this free analysis, offered without any obligation on your part.

Yours truly,

_____

Enclosure: [*Card*]

NOTE: *Employee newsletters are an excellent source of retiree information. Some personnel offices also provide this information. You could enclose the Free Market Analysis Certificate on page 24 with this letter. If you are mailing a listing solicitation letter to someone who may have already listed his or her home, we recommend adding the following statement to the end of the letter: "If you have already listed your home for sale with your broker, please disregard this letter."*

Free Market Analysis Certificate

Free Market Analysis

This certificate is good for one free computer-generated comparative market analysis indicating the likely sales price you could expect to receive for your home in today's marketplace.

This analysis is provided without any charge or obligation on your part to list or sell your home.

⌈ *Bob Jones* ⌉
⌊ *Clyde Realty* ⌋   [*555-8200*]

　　　　　Evenings: [*555-6188*]

NOTE: This certificate can be mailed to For-Sale-by-Owner families as well as to potential clients in general. It can also be used as an enclosure or flyer.

A Neighbor Listed with Us

[*Date*]

_____

_____

_____

Dear _____ :

Do you

Want To Know What Your Neighbors Did?

Your neighbors [*John and Mary Smith*] at [*111 Midvale Lane*] have just placed their home for sale through [*Clyde Realty*].

They will be able to take advantage of [*the exceptional demand our office has been experiencing in your area / the current seller's market / the rapid appreciation in value of the past few years / the recent upturn in the real estate market*].

If you want to know what a sale of your home can mean for you in dollars and common sense, I can provide you with a computer-generated market analysis showing you what you can expect from a sale of your home. This service is provided at no cost or obligation.

I will call you in the next few days to find out if you want to take advantage of this offer and to ask for your help in choosing a new neighbor.

Yours truly,

_____

Enclosure: [*Card*]

NOTE: *Be sure to obtain permission from the seller before you send out this letter. You could include the Free Market Analysis Certificate on page 24 with this letter. Besides soliciting listings, this letter lets neighbors know property* *is available and it can serve to locate buyers. If you are mailing a listing solicitation letter to someone who may have already listed his or her home, we recommend adding the following statement to the end of the letter: "If you have already listed your home for sale with your broker, please disregard this letter."*

What's Happening in Your Neighborhood?

[*Date*]

_____

_____

_____

Dear _____ :

Do you know what's happening in your neighborhood?

We Are Zeroing In on Your Home!

The following properties have been recently sold [*around your home*] [*by Clyde Realty*].

[*3BR Stardust Lane*]	[*$189,500*]
[*2BR Stardust Circle*]	[*$167,500*]
[*3BR Lynn Court*]	[*$214,500*]
[*4BR Lynn Court*]	[*$274,500*]

Would *you* like to see a "Sold" sign in front of your property as well?

I will be calling you in the next few days to find out if you would like to receive a free, no-obligation, comparative market analysis indicating what you can expect to receive from a sale of your home.

Yours truly,

_____

Enclosure: [*Card*]

NOTE: *Consider enclosing the Free Market Analysis Certificate on page 24 with this flyer. Do not give exact addresses of particular homes without permission of both buyer and seller. If you are mailing a listing solicitation letter to someone who may have already listed his or her home, we recommend adding the following statement to the end of the letter: "If you have already listed your home for sale with your broker, please disregard this letter."*

Farewell to Your Old Neighbors—
Welcome to the New Ones!

[*Date*]

_____

_____

_____

Dear _____ :

Farewell to Your Old Neighbors—Welcome to the New Ones!

It must seem that you have said goodbye to many old neighbors; [*Clyde Realty*] has sold [*19*] homes in [*Truesdale Estates*] in the last [*6*] months. On the bright side, you have the opportunity to make many new friends.

There are good reasons for our phenomenal success in [*Truesdale Estates*], and I would like the opportunity to discuss them with you.

I would also like to prepare a comparative market analysis that indicates the likely sales price of your home in today's marketplace should you decide to sell. We perform this service without *any* cost or obligation on your part!

I will call you in a few days to see if I can assist you with your real estate needs.

Yours truly,

_____

Enclosure: [*Card*]

NOTE: *You could include the Free Market Analysis Certificate on page 24 with this letter If you are mailing a listing solicitation letter to someone who may have already listed his or her home, we recommend adding the following statement to the end of the letter: "If you have already listed your home for sale with your broker, please disregard this letter."*

We Move Houses

[*Date*]

_____

_____

_____

Dear _____ :

Did you know that

We Move Houses? (No Size Limit)

We can find a new owner for your home and, if you wish, have you in a new home in record time.

Want to know how we do it? The answer is with a lot of hard work. We develop a marketing plan for a property and then work the plan.

I will be calling you in the next few days to tell you more about our marketing plan and to offer you a computer-generated comparative market analysis that indicates what you will likely receive from the sale of your home in today's marketplace. This service is provided free, without any obligation on your part.

Yours truly,

_____

Enclosure: [*Card*]

NOTE: *You could enclose the Free Market Analysis Certificate on page 24 with this letter. If you are mailing a listing solicitation letter to someone who may have already listed his or her home, we recommend adding the following statement to the end of the letter: "If you haave already listed your home for sale with your broker, please disregard this letter."*

Help Us Find a Home for a Neighbor #1

[*Date*]

_____

_____

_____

Dear _____ :

Can You Help a Neighbor?

We need a 3-bedroom home in your neighborhood for a [*young family*]. The [*husband is an engineer, and the wife is a schoolteacher. They have a son 11 years old and a daughter who is 7. They would like to relocate prior to school in September and desire a home within walking distance of Midvale School*].

I will be calling you in a few days to determine if you know of anyone in the neighborhood who might consider selling their home to this fine family.

Sincerely,

_____

Enclosure: [*Card*]

NOTE: *The heading should get this letter read. The prospective buyers should be real people with whom you are working, and they should be pictured in a very positive manner. People will go out of their way to help specific people, but not people in general.*

This is not only an effective listing canvassing tool, but the effort expended for the buyers you are working for will serve to make them feel indebted to you, reducing the chances of their contacting other agents.

Help Us Find a Home for a Neighbor #2

[*Date*]

_____

_____

_____

Dear _____ :

We are desperately looking for a [*three-bedroom, two-bath*] home
[*close to / within walking distance of / within golfcart distance of*]
[*the First Midvale Congregational Church / the Palm Dale Country
Club*]. The home is needed for a [*young family who have a son
9 years old and a daughter 7 years old. They are transferring to
the area and would like to become members of your church*].

I will be calling you in the next few days to ask for any suggestions
you can provide in helping us find a home for this fine family.

Yours truly,

_____

Enclosure: [*Card*]

NOTE: *You want to picture the buyers you are working with in a
very positive fashion. People like to help nice people, especially when they have common interests. This solicitation is
extremely effective when mailed to the membership of a
particular group, such as golf clubs, health clubs, specific
companies, and so on. By using your buyer's interests, you
can target people within the desired area who have similar
interests. Because this solicitation is so effective, you
should consider asking prospective buyers if they prefer to
locate within walking distance of any particular religious
institution, club, or the like. By contacting the group, you
should be able to obtain a membership list. A letter such as
this also serves to obligate the buyers.*

Listing Solicitation—Out-of-Town Owner

[*Date*]

_____

_____

_____

Dear _____ :

As you undoubtedly know, owning property that is located far away from you can be a real hassle.

[*Right now, we are experiencing an exceptional market.*] [*Despite current market conditions, we are selling property.*] I believe that we can sell your [*three-bedroom home*] in [*Midvale Heights*] at an attractive price. In fact, we would be happy to prepare, without cost or obligation, a comparative market analysis to show you what you could expect to receive from a sale in the present market.

I will be calling you in the next few days to ascertain your interests in selling your property.

Yours truly,

_____

Enclosure: [*Card*]

NOTE: *The knowledge of an imminent call makes an owner consider the option of selling. This letter has greater effect if the property has vacancies, needs repair or has had recent evictions. You could enclose the Free Market Analysis Certificate on page 24 with this letter. If you are mailing a listing solicitation letter to someone who may have already listed his or her home, we recommend adding the following statement to the end of the letter: "If you have already listed your home for sale with your broker, please disregard this letter."*

Listing Solicitation—Apartments

[*Date*]

_____

_____

_____

Dear _____ :

Tenant Problems?

Have you considered the advantage of having your apartment equity in management-free government bonds, tax-free municipals, or . . . ?

- No rents to try to collect!
- No vacancies to worry about!
- No repairs to make!
- No tenant complaints!
- No building inspector problems!
- No evictions!

I will be calling you in a few days to determine your interest in selling. (If you are happy as a landlord, we can even sell you another building.)

Incidentally, we perform a computer-generated comparative market analysis, at no cost or obligation to you, that indicates what you can expect to receive from the sale of your apartment building.

Yours truly,

_____

Enclosure: [*Card*]

NOTE: *Besides general mailings to owners of apartments, consider checking public records for problem property for* *evictions, unpaid taxes, code violations, and so on. You could enclose the Free Market Analysis Certificate on page 24 with this letter.*

If you are mailing a listing solicitation letter to someone who may have already listed his or her property, we recommend adding the following statement to the end of the letter: "If you have already listed your property for sale with your broker, please disregard this letter."

Builder Solicitation—Building Permit

[*Date*]

_____

_____

_____

Dear _____ :

I was happy to learn that you have taken out a construction permit for another new home at [_____]. The area has been developing well, and we have had excellent sales activity in the neighborhood.

I believe the most effective new-home marketing effort really starts before construction begins. A plan review by a marketing specialist often reveals that some costly features are not essential, while other features can increase the home's salability and sales price far beyond their additional cost. I will be calling you in a few days to schedule a meeting so we can discuss ways to ensure a quick sale and to maximize your profits as well.

Yours truly,

_____

Enclosure: [*Card*]

NOTE: *Send this letter for building permits taken out in the builder's name. Homes being built for a buyer usually have the permit in the buyer's name.*

This letter offers benefits to the reader. Mentioning an impending call encourages the reader to review the plan features, which is a benefit to the builder.

Chapter

3

Responses to Owner Inquiries

Response to Value Inquiry #1

[*Date*]

_____

_____

_____

Dear _____ :

Regarding your inquiry about the value of your [*lot / home / building*] at [_____], I believe the current market would support a sales price in the [*$* _____] to [*$* _____] range.

[*This value estimate is based on* (list positive and/or negative attributes of the property) *and the recent sales of* (give address) *for* ($ _____), (supply address) *for* ($ _____), *and* (supply address) *for* ($ _____).]

[*The value is based on the enclosed comparative market analysis and the fact that your home has* (list features influencing value).]

Because of the current market conditions, I recommend a list price of $ _____ and I have enclosed an agency agreement reflecting this price. Please sign and return [*two*] copies to our office so we can begin our efforts to obtain a buyer for your [*lot / home / building*].

Yours truly,

_____

Enclosures: [*Card*] [*Comparative Market Analysis*] [*Agency Agreement*]

NOTE: *Do not give out information concerning sales without the permission of buyers and sellers.*

This letter was written for owners who are not available for a personal meeting.

The positive features should show that you can appreciate the property's benefits. Don't be picky about the negative features, but list some of them when you are certain that the owner realizes they are present.

Whenever you want the recipient to mail an enclosure back to you, include a self-addressed envelope, preferably with prepaid postage.

The last paragraph assumes that the owner will list the property. By reading this assumption and the instructions, owners often comply.

This letter should be followed up with a phone call several days after its receipt.

Response to Value Inquiry #2

[*Date*]

_____

_____

_____

Dear _____ :

In response to your inquiry about the value of your property at [*111 Midvale Lane*], I have performed a comparative market analysis. The analysis shows recent sales of similar properties, similar properties currently on the market and similar properties that were not sold at their listed prices. Based on the enclosed comparative market analysis, I recommend that your property be placed on the market at [*$175,000*]. I have also included agency agreements reflecting this price.

I believe it is a particularly advantageous time to place your property on the market because of [*the increase in sales activity / the opportunity to lock in the recent appreciation in value / the current higher interest rates, which make seller financing so attractive / the current low interest rates / the present demand for homes in the area*]. Please sign and return [*two*] copies of the agency agreement, and we will immediately get to work on marketing your [*three-bedroom home*].

I will be calling you in the next few days to answer any questions that you might have.

Yours truly,

_____

Enclosures: [*Card*] [*Comparative Market Analysis*] [*Agency Agreement*]

NOTE: *The term* agency agreement *has a benefit connotation. Listing often has a negative connotation because the word is associated with commission rather than with benefits. See notes in previous letter.*

Response to Value Inquiry #3

[*Date*]

_____

_____

_____

Dear _____ :

[*$46,000*] cash is our estimate of what you will have after paying off the mortgage and all sales costs for a sale of your home at [_____].

This estimate is based on the enclosed computer-generated comparative market analysis indicating that your home should sell for [*$149,000*]. The enclosed seller's proceeds estimate shows the estimated deductions from the gross sales price to arrive at the net.

I have also enclosed agency agreements reflecting the [*$149,000*] sale price. If [*$46,000*] cash interests you, please sign and return [*two*] copies of the agreements to our office so we can immediately get to work on selling your home [*and take advantage of this favorable market*].

I will be calling you in a few days to answer any questions that you might have.

Yours truly,

_____

Enclosures

NOTE: *Like the prior two letters, a value inquiry should be answered by mail only when the owner is not available for a personal presentation.*

Response to Value Inquiry—
Poor Market Conditions

[*Date*]

_____

_____

_____

Dear _____ :

At the present time, the number of homesellers far exceeds that of
homebuyers for [*state type of property*]. Unless you must sell, I
recommend that you keep the property off the market at this time.

If you must sell, you will have to give your property a competitive
edge. Similar property is currently listed between [$ _____]
and [$ _____] but not selling well even at the lower prices.
The enclosed comparative market analysis confirms this. Therefore,
I recommend an even lower listing price of [$_____]. Such
a price will attract attention and is likely to result in a sale even
under our present market conditions.

I have enclosed an agency agreement for your property reflecting
the above price. Please sign and return [*two*] copies if you wish to
sell your property at this time. I will call you in a few days to
answer any questions that you might have.

Yours truly,

_____

Enclosures: [*Comparative market analysis, Agency agreement*]

NOTE: *This letter's strength is its honesty. It will be a salable
listing if you get it—not one likely to cost you money. This
suggestion of delay is an effective negative approach when
you know the seller will be taking a loss. Call the owner to
discuss your evaluation if you do not receive a response
within ten days.*

Response to Value Inquiry—Repairs Needed

[*Date*]

_____

_____

_____

Dear _____ :

I have carefully examined your home at [_____]. The resulting comparative market analysis is enclosed.

While I am confident that I will be able to find a buyer at the price indicated in my analysis, I think you should seriously consider some property repairs. I believe approximately [$ _____] in repairs could result in an increase in the selling price of [$ _____]. I recommend these repairs:

[*1. Paint exterior.*]

[*2. Repair porch and railing.*]

[*3. Paint living room and kitchen (light colors).*]

[*4. Install new lighting fixture in kitchen.*]

[*5. Replace floor tile in bath.*]

[*6. Hang vinyl wall covering in bath.*]

[*7. Professionally clean carpets.*]

I would be happy to obtain bids for all the work and also to assist you in obtaining any desired financing.

I have enclosed an agency agreement for the property, based on selling the property without any repairs. Please sign and return [*two*] copies. If you decide to go ahead with the repairs and improvements, we can adjust the price to reflect the improvements.

I will call you in a few days to answer any questions that you might have.

Yours truly,

_____

Enclosures: [*Comparative market analysis, Agency agreement*]

NOTE: *The choice is not whether to sign a listing or not, but whether to make repairs or sell the property "as is."*

About Our Firm

[*Date*]

_____

_____

_____

Dear _____ :

In answer to your inquiry about [*Clyde Realty*], I would like to tell you about our firm:

[*We have been in business for 26 years. / I have been engaged in the real estate business since 1970.*] [*We are one of the largest firms in the area, with 56 salespeople in three offices. / We are a small firm specializing in (describe specialty).*]

[*As a member in good standing of the (Pineview) Multiple Listing Service, we are able to make your home available to (118) offices and more than (600) salespeople.*] [*Our success record has been exemplary over the past few years and (based on the present market,) I expect continued success for the future.*]

[*I have enclosed a comparative market analysis prepared for your home, showing what you could expect to receive at a sale. Also enclosed is an agency agreement reflecting our recommended sale price. Please sign and return (two) copies of the agreement to us if you would like our firm to arrange a sale of your property.*]

I will call you in the next few days to see if you have any further questions.

Yours truly,

_____

Enclosures: [*Comparative market analysis, Agency agreement*]

Listing and Management—Apartment

[*Date*]

_____
_____
_____

Dear _____ :

I have completed an in-depth analysis of your apartment building at
[_____]. The enclosed comparative market analysis is
based on these changes:

[*1. Raising the rents of units one, three and seven an additional $40
per month and raising the rents of units four, six, eight and ten $20
per month. These rents are currently below market level.*]

[*2. Painting vacant units five and nine as well as replacing carpeting.*]

[*3. Painting the exterior and performing needed landscaping work,
including planting flowers.*]

We would be happy to take charge of all required work. Enclosed is
a property management agreement as well as an agency agreement.
Please sign and return [*two*] copies of each so that we can immediately start preparing your property for a favorable sale.

I will contact you within the next few days to answer any questions
that you might have.

Yours truly,

_____

Enclosures: [*Comparative market analysis, Property management
agreement, agency agreement*]

NOTE: *When you sell apartments, having management authority
will allow you to make the property more salable and
increase your likelihood of success.*

Referral of Inquiry

[*Date*]

_____

_____

_____

Dear _____ :

I appreciate your considering [*Clyde Realty*] for marketing your property at [_____].

However, because [*of the distance from our office / we specialize in residential property*], it would not be fair to you if we market your property. You need a broker who [*is more familiar with the area / specializes in marketing rental property*].

We have contacted [*Lynn Jones*] at [*Jones Realty*] about your property. Because of their [*location / experience in marketing rental property*], I believe they can better meet your needs. [*Lynn Jones*] will be contacting you in the next few days.

[*We have successfully referred buyers and sellers to (Lynn Jones) in the past and feel certain that she will be able to help you. / (Jones Realty) is a member of (Refer-All, Inc.), the referral service to which we belong. Because the members are all trained professionals, I feel certain that they will be able to help you.*]

Again, thank you for considering [*Clyde Realty*]. If we can serve you in the future, please feel free to contact me at [*555-1111*].

Yours truly,

_____

Enclosure: [*Card*]

NOTE: *This letter treats a value inquiry as an offer of a listing. It increases the likelihood that the referral firm will be able to obtain an agency agreement.*

Refusal of Open Listing

[*Date*]

_____

_____

_____

Dear _____ :

Thank you very much for offering our firm an open listing on your property at [_____]. We must, however, decline your kind offer. Our acceptance of an open listing would not be fair to you.

Experience has shown that property that is not listed exclusively seldom sells. No one advertises it, and the property will be shown only when an agent doesn't have an exclusive agency property to fit a buyer's needs. Accepting such a listing would mean deceiving you and giving you a false hope for sales success.

I have therefore included an exclusive-right-to-sell agency agreement making [*Clyde Realty*] responsible for selling your [*home*]. If you are serious about wishing to sell, please sign and return [*two*] copies of the agreement.

I will be calling you within the next few days to answer any questions and to tell you about our marketing plan for your [*home*].

Yours truly,

_____

Enclosures: [*Card, Exclusive-right-to-sell agency agreement*]

NOTE: *You may also wish to include a comparative market analysis. To many, the term* agency agreement *creates an image of a helpful partnership, while* listing *carries a more negative connotation.*

Chapter

4

Solicitations for For Sale by Owner Listings

The Owner's Quiz

[*Date*]

_____

_____

_____

Dear _____ :

Can You Pass the Owner's Quiz?

- Do you have a buyer?
- Have you qualified him or her on financial ability?
- Is your buyer contractually obligated to the purchase?
- Has your buyer been able to arrange the necessary financing?

If all the answers are yes, then congratulations on your sale! If you answered no to any of these questions, you have not yet sold your home.

I will call you in the next few days to find out how you scored and to show you how [*Clyde Realty*] can sell your home without any cost to you.

Yours truly,

_____

Enclosure: [*Card*]

NOTE: *You may wish to use one of the approaches from* Power Real Estate Listing [*Real Estate Education Company*] *to show the client how the buyer, not the seller, really pays the commission.*

Use reverse directories to obtain owners' names from addresses or telephone numbers. You can also locate an owner from the office of your tax assessor or your local title company. Never address a letter "To Occupant"!

Full-Price Buyer

[*Date*]

_____

_____

_____

Dear _____ :

If I had a full-price buyer for your home, would you be willing to pay our fee?

I will call you to find out if your answer is "Yes"!

Yours truly,

_____

Enclosure: [*Card*]

NOTE: *This short note will generally result in owner interest. It provides a chance to be invited to view the premises and to talk to the owner. Remember, you have not said you have a buyer; you only asked if the owner would pay a fee if you had one.*

Agents Sell

[*Date*]

_____
_____
_____

Dear _____ :

Why For Sale by Owner Signs Get Replaced by Agent Signs: Because Agents Sell!

Utilizing an agent means:

- You are protected against unscrupulous buyers hoping to pay less than market value for your home.
- No unescorted, unqualified persons will enter your home.
- Contracts are likely to end in a sale—not in a courtroom.
- You are able to meet buyer financing needs.
- You are no longer a prisoner in your own home waiting for the bell to ring.
- You are more likely to sell your home.
- The sale will result in a higher net profit.

Please think about it. I will call you in the next few days to answer any questions you might have and to prove that everything I have told you is true.

Yours truly,

_____

Enclosure: [*Card*]

No Agent

[*Date*]

_____

_____

_____

Dear _____ :

You probably know that

No Agent = No Commission

That seems like a good reason to try to sell without an agent except that "no agent" all too often means "no sale." That explains why so many For Sale by Owner signs are replaced by agent signs.

I will call you in the next few days to show you not only the dangers of owner sales but also the positive benefits we can offer. If I show you how I can put more money in your pockets, will you want to talk with me?

Yours truly,

_____

Enclosure: [*Card*]

NOTE: *This is a short, effective letter. It grabs the reader's attention and states a common owner belief. Asking if the reader will talk to you to find out how to make more money from the sale of a home makes it hard to say no. When you call, you might say, "[Mr. Smith], I wrote you the other day and told you I would call. I asked whether you would talk with me if I show you how I could put more money in your pockets. I would like to show* [you and your spouse] *how I will accomplish this. Will* [you and your spouse] *be home* [tonight at 7:00 PM], *or would* [8:00 PM] *be more convenient?"*

You are giving them a choice about when *to talk,* not whether *they will talk with you. When you meet them, you can use strategies from* Power Real Estate Listing *(Chicago: Real Estate Education Company), to show the seller the financial benefits of listing with your office.*

Free Help

[*Date*]

_____

_____

_____

Dear _____ :

Can you use some free help?

Our office supplies [*purchase offer forms* / *For Sale by Owner suggestions*] to owners who wish to sell their homes without the use of an agent. We do so without cost or obligation. We also provide a free estimate of value based on current documented sales.

No, we are not a charity—we do this hoping that if you later decide to use an agent's services, you will remember our assistance.

I will call you within the next few days to set up an appointment so I can drop off the [*forms* / *information*] with you and answer any questions you might have.

Yours truly,

_____

Enclosure: [*Card*]

NOTE: *The free offer is an effective door-opener. By explaining how the forms are to be filled out, with appropriate warnings, mandatory disclosures, applications for financing, qualifying ratios, and so on, the owner will begin to understand that selling a home is more complicated than just finding a buyer. You should then be in a position to discuss the benefits of having professional representation.*

Selling Without an Agent

[*Date*]

_____

_____

_____

Dear _____ :

Are you

Selling Without an Agent?
You Can Do It, But BE CAREFUL!

I have enclosed a group of helpful hints and warnings that we have compiled to help owners who don't wish to use an agent. Study them carefully. Not only can they mean the difference between a sale and no sale; they can also protect you against a lawsuit or losing your home to an unscrupulous buyer.

If you want an explanation of any of this material or would like to know how you could benefit financially and emotionally from being represented by an agent, please contact me.

I will check with you in a few days to see how you are doing and to offer whatever advice I can.

Yours truly,

_____

Enclosures: ["How To Sell Your Home Without an Agent" can be adapted as an enclosure (see pages 61–63).]

The Sign in Front of Your Home

[*Date*]

_____

_____

_____

Dear _____ :

SOLD!

Is this the sign in front of your home? Or is it simply,

For Sale by Owner

The likelihood of turning the second sign into the first sign is very slim, which explains why so many For Sale by Owner signs are replaced by broker's signs.

Do you realize that:

1. Most calls on For Sale by Owner signs come from people who can't afford the home they are calling about?

2. Most calls from newspaper ads are from people who would not be satisfied with a home priced in the range they inquired about?

Without having a variety of homes to match inquiries, most of an owner's efforts end up wasted.

I will call you in the next few days, not to try to saddle you with agent selling fees but to show you how I can help you have more money in your pocket after a sale.

Isn't what you actually net more important than anything else?

Yours truly,

_____

Enclosure: [*Card*]

How to Sell Without an Agent

[*Date*]

_____

_____

_____

Dear _____ :

Want some help on

How To Sell Your Home Without an Agent?

1. **Change ads regularly.** Ads lose their effectiveness if repeated without change. Three days is plenty for one ad. Rewrite ads to appeal to different categories of likely buyers. Use plenty of adjectives. Spend time writing good copy, because your ad competes with many ads for similar property.

2. **Obtain purchase contract forms.** (Call our office if you do not have any). Complete the purchase contract except for date, price, terms and signatures. Make certain that you fully understand every provision. If a prospective buyer wants to use his or her own contract, be alert. Take it to an attorney. What might appear to be a standard form could be one-sided and not say what it appears at first reading to say. With desktop publishing, many wheeler-dealers are using their own forms where the small print taketh away what the large print giveth!

3. **Check financing at least once a week with a mortgage company so you will be able to help a buyer understand his or her down payment and monthly costs for various types of mortgages tailored to the buyer's needs.** You will need to buy an amortization table from your local bookstore. Be prepared to explain loan types to prospective buyers. Many excellent texts are available to help you. You must also understand front-end and back-end qualifying ratios. If you don't understand them, you could waste months of effort on a buyer who is unable to obtain financing because of existing debt or insufficient income.

4. **If a prospective buyer uses the words *subordinate* or *subordination* in the offer, turn and run.** If you sign, no matter how good it looks, you are likely giving away your home to

a charlatan. Also, be alert for any deals that seem too good to be true—they generally are. Be particularly wary with any buyer who is buying without any of his or her own cash. If the buyer ends up with more cash than he or she started with, you can be certain you are the victim of a scam. A number of fast-talking seminar promoters have instructed thousands in unethical and often illegal procedures. Offers of mortgages on other property, notes, colored stones, diamonds (especially uncut) or other claimed valuables should send you running to an attorney. If you don't have one, I would be happy to recommend several. When an agent is involved, the fast operators don't waste their time. That's why they *love* For Sale by Owners.

5. **Be certain that you have considered and fully understand the effects of the following:** seller discount points, payoff penalties on existing loans, assumability of loans, ownership of the impound account and advantages of having fire insurance policies assumed rather than a short-rate cancellation. You should also understand the dangers of "subject-to" financing as opposed to loan assumptions.

6. **Make certain that you are prepared with all seller disclosures mandated by state law.** If you are not prepared, you may not be able to obligate a buyer to a sale.

7. **Make certain that you fully understand the requirements of state and federal fair housing legislation,** or you could find yourself paying a fine or a penalty.

8. **Make certain you know who a prospective buyer is before he or she crosses your threshold.** There have been far too many horror cases of trusting homeowners who open their homes to persons with intentions other than buying, and treat them as if they were honored guests. Try not to be alone when prospective buyers visit.

9. **Beware of contingent offers.** As a result of a contingency, the property could be tied up for months or even years. The buyer could be a dealer who wants to hold the property as if it were an option that would be exercised only if another buyer is located.

10. **How did you arrive at your price?** Unless you have a written comparative market analysis that considers all recent sales of comparable property, your price could be merely a hunch. Too high a price will almost certainly guarantee that

your property will not be sold, and you will be simply wasting time and effort. Too low a price will mean you are giving away dollars that are rightfully yours. You want a realistic price that gives you an advantage over your competition in creating interest in your property. You should then hold to your price with only minor concessions.

11. **Understand fully the tax consequences of the sale.** Have you considered the advantages of a tax-free exchange where you choose the property you receive? Have you considered the tax benefit of providing some seller financing on an installment sale?

If you are determined to sell your home yourself, we wish you good luck. I will, however, be contacting you in the next few days to discuss some of the advantages of having agency representation that you may not have considered.

Yours truly,

_____

Enclosure: [*Card*]

NOTE: *This letter can also be adapted as a handout or as an enclosure with other For Sale by Owner letters.*

Even though the letter is long, it will be read, as it appears to be offering benefits.

Owners Who Have Homes for Rent

[*Date*]

_____

_____

_____

Dear _____ :

Do You Really Want To Rent?

Consider these points:

- Rental income seldom makes economic sense when compared to the likely sale price.
- When you rent your home, you are placing a tenant in charge of a valuable asset. Consider the dangers of a careless tenant.

Let us show you how we can sell your home now and what you could expect to receive from a sale. We can furnish a computer-generated market analysis without any cost or obligation on your part.

I will be contacting you in the next few days to discuss the advantages that a sale offers you over renting.

Yours truly,

_____

Enclosure: [*Card*]

Unsuccessful Listing Attempt #1

[*Date*]

_____

_____

_____

Dear _____ :

Thank you very much for the opportunity to visit your home in [*Westwood*]. As I indicated, I believe that [*Clyde Realty*] can help you find the perfect family who will appreciate all your home has to offer.

I will be contacting you again in a few weeks to check on your sale progress and to find out how I can help you in your efforts.

Yours truly,

_____

Enclosure: [*Card*]

Unsuccessful Listing Attempt #2

[*Date*]

_____

_____

_____

Dear _____ :

I would like to thank you for the opportunity to view your home [*this past Thursday*]. I am certain that, if you give us the opportunity, we could find a buyer for your home who is willing to pay a reasonable value.

If you have any questions about selling your home, please do not hesitate to contact me. I will call you again in about a week to see how your efforts are going.

Yours truly,

_____

Enclosure: [*Card*]

NOTE: *A good time for a personal follow-up contact is late Sunday afternoon after an unsuccessful owner open house!*

Chapter

5

Servicing
the Listing

Thank You for Listing #1

[*Date*]

_____

_____

_____

Dear _____ :

As the broker with [*Clyde Realty*], I appreciate the confidence you
have shown by making [*Clyde Realty*] your exclusive agent for the
sale of your home.

I want you to know that we will use our best efforts to locate a
buyer at the highest price and best terms possible for you. Besides
our own sales force, other agents will have access to your home
through our multiple-listing service; in effect, you will have [*107*]
offices and [*852*] salespeople working on your behalf.

[*Janet Jones*] will keep in contact with you about advertising, showings and suggestions for increasing the salability of your home. If
you have any questions at all, please call [*him / her*] or me.

I look forward to meeting your needs with a completed sale.

Yours truly,

_____

Enclosure: [*Card*]

Thank You for Listing #2

[*Date*]

———————————

———————————

———————————

Dear ——————— :

I appreciate the trust you have shown in [*Clyde Realty*] by appointing us your agent for the sale of your [*home*].

I want you to know you can expect us to be diligent and professional in our efforts to make a favorable sale on your [*home*]. We have already [*prepared initial advertising / placed initial advertising*] and provided information on your home to [*our multiple-listing service*]. We will keep you up-to-date on our progress. [*Mr. Lynn Smith*] of our office will be working with you throughout the sales process and even after the sale to ensure a satisfactory closing. If you have any questions concerning your property or our efforts, please contact [*Mr. Smith*].

I look forward to presenting you with a buyer.

Yours truly,

———————————

Enclosure: [*Card*]

Thank You for Listing—Out-of-Town Owner

[*Date*]

_____

_____

_____

Dear _____ :

I would like to thank you for showing your confidence in [*Clyde Realty*] by appointing us your exclusive agent for the sale of your property. We have already entered your [*home*] on the multiple-listing service computer. Your [*home*] is now available to [*712*] agents in [*57*] offices.

Because you live a great distance from our office, would you please provide us with the following information?

1. The name and phone number of a local person to contact in the event of an emergency

2. The name and address of your property insurance agent and policy number

3. The name and phone number of your local attorney (if applicable)

You should contact your insurance agent to make certain that you have adequate coverage.

I look forward to telling you that your [*home*] has been sold.

Sincerely,

_____

Enclosure: [*Card*]

Neighborhood Information Request

[*Date*]

_____

_____

_____

Dear _____ :

Having an in-depth knowledge of your neighborhood and neighbors can give us a competitive edge over less informed sales agents who represent other properties.

We value your knowledge of your community and would therefore appreciate if you would share this knowledge by completing this form to the best of your ability to help us sell your home.

1. Neighborhood features you feel a buyer would be most pleased with: _____

2. School districts: _____

3. School bus stops: _____

4. Names, ages and schools attended by neighborhood children (include private schools):

   _____   _____   _____

   _____   _____   _____

   _____   _____   _____

   _____   _____   _____

   _____   _____   _____

5. Youth activities in the area (Little League, junior hockey, soccer league, etc.): _____

6. Public recreational facilities in the area (parks, pools, playgrounds, tennis courts, etc.): _____

7. Nearest public transportation route: _____

8. Nearest medical facility: _____

9. Nearest community center (for children, seniors, etc.):

   _____

10. Nearest houses of worship: _____

11. Nearest shopping area: _____

12. General information on closest neighbors: _____

    _____

13. The professions of people living in area that might interest a possible buyer (doctor, banker, attorney, professor or another professional): _____

14. Describe the interests of the person or family you feel would best appreciate your home and neighborhood:

    _____

15. Other information that would be of interest to a likely buyer:

    _____

Please send your completed form to my attention in the enclosed postage-paid envelope.

We greatly appreciate your help in providing this information about your neighborhood.

Appreciatively yours,

_____

Enclosure: [*Card*]

_____

NOTE: *Not only does this letter gain you sales ammunition, it also shows the owner that you appreciate the neighborhood and neighbors and are making your best efforts on their behalf.*

Instruction Sheet Transmittal

[*Date*]

_____

_____

_____

Dear _____ :

In marketing your home, we are competing against [*dozens / hundreds*] of other owners who are all after a much smaller pool of buyers. To compete successfully, we want to gain every possible advantage. The enclosed instruction sheet allows you to play an important role in obtaining the best possible sale for your home.

Thank you very much. Please call me if you have any questions.

Yours truly,

_____

Enclosures: [*Homeowner instructions, Card*]

Homeowner Instructions

Homeowner Hints for a Successful Sale

I. Exterior

    A. **Grass and shrubs.** Keep trimmed. Consider a fast-greening fertilizer such as ammonium sulfate (inexpensive) for a deep green lawn.

    B. **Pets.** If you have a dog, clean up any dog dirt on a daily basis. Secure pets while the house is being shown. If you have a cat, change the litter box daily.

    C. **Fences.** Make any needed repairs. A neat, well-painted fence gives a positive impression.

    D. **Flowers.** Plant seasonal blooming flowers, especially near the front door and in any patio area. A profusion of color can have your home half-sold before the door is even opened.

    E. **Bird feeders.** Hummingbird feeders and bird houses create a pleasant mood, especially when they are close to any patio area.

    F. **Paint.**

        1. **Front door.** Front door should be refinished or painted if it shows excessive wear.

        2. **Condition of exterior paint.** Often only the trim or, depending on sun exposure, only one or two sides of the house need painting. Keep in mind that paint is cheap compared to the extra dollars a home with a clean, fresh appearance will bring.

    G. **Lawn furniture.** Place lawn furniture in an attractive, leisurely manner. A badminton net or croquet set-up gives a positive image as well.

H. **Roof.** If the roof needs to be repaired or re-placed, it's best to have the work done. Other-wise, buyers will want to deduct the cost even if your price already reflects the required work. Delaying repairs can actually cost you twice as much.

II. Interior

A. **Housekeeping.** You are competing against model homes, so your home must look as much like a model as possible. Floors, bath fixtures and appliances must be sparkling. Consider using a car wax on appliances. Make beds early in the day. Unmade beds and late sleepers cre-ate a very negative image.

B. **Odors and aromas.** Avoid heavy frying, using vinegar or cooking strong-smelling foods such as cabbage. The odors last and work against the image you are trying to create. On the other hand, some smells have a positive effect on people: Baked bread, apple pie, chocolate cook-ies and cinnamon rolls are examples of foods that can help sell your home. Consider keeping packaged cookie or bread dough in the refriger-ator. Just before a scheduled showing, the smell of these baking foods can be a great help to us. If you or your family members smoke, don't smoke in your home and don't allow guests to smoke. Stale tobacco odors can be masked with some odor sprays. If the temperature allows it, open windows and air out the house every morning.

C. **Paint.** If you have leftover paint, you can accom-plish a great deal by doing touch-ups where needed. If the surface is dark, repaint with light colors such as off-white, oyster, light beige or pale yellow. Light colors make rooms appear fresh as well as larger.

D. **Plumbing.** Repair any leaky faucets. Make certain that you don't have a gurgling toilet.

E. **Shades and blinds.** Replace any torn shades or broken blinds.

F. **Drapes.** If drapes need cleaning, have it done. If they are old and worn, stained or dark, consider replacing them with either light-colored drapes or off-white vinyl vertical blinds. (Large department stores or catalog houses usually have standard sizes.)

G. **Carpets.** Dirty carpets should be either professionally steam-cleaned (preferred), or you should rent a heavy-duty cleaner. If the carpet is badly worn, replace it with new carpet (and a quality pad) in a neutral color. Consider either a plush or berber carpet.

H. **Lighting.** If any room appears dark, increase the wattage of your light bulbs. Before a showing, open the blinds and drapes and turn on the lights, even during the day—you want the house as bright as possible. Be sure that your light fixtures and windows are clean.

I. **Closets.** If closets appear crowded, remove items not needed and put in boxes. They can be stacked neatly in a corner of the basement, attic or garage.

J. **Too much furniture.** Many homes appear crowded, with too many pieces of large furniture and too much bric-a-brac. Consider putting excess furniture in a storage locker.

K. **Garage and basement.** Spruce up your work area. Consider a garage sale to get rid of items you no longer need. Put excess items in boxes and stack them neatly in a corner. Consider using a commercial garage floor cleaner on oil and grease marks on the garage floor and driveway. You might consider a commercial steam cleaner (not a carpet cleaner).

L. **Temperature.** On cold days, a natural fire in the fireplace will help us sell your home. Start the fire before the showing is scheduled. On hot days, consider turning the air conditioner four to five degrees cooler than normal. The contrast will seem phenomenal, making a very positive impression. In moderate weather, open windows for fresh air.

III.   Your Best Role during Showings

When your home is shown, it's best that you disappear for a while. Buyers feel restrained with an owner present. If buyers hesitate to voice their concerns, then their questions cannot be answered and their problems cannot be solved.

If you must remain in the house, try to stay in one area. Excellent places to be are working in the garden, on the lawn or in the workshop. These activities create a positive image. While soft music is fine, turn off the TV.

Never, never follow the agent around the house during the showing, volunteer any information or answer questions the buyers may have. You have engaged professional real estate salespeople. We will ask you questions if necessary.

$\begin{bmatrix} \textit{Clyde Realty} \\ \textit{555-8200} \end{bmatrix}$

NOTE: *Besides using these instructions as an enclosure with a letter, you can also use it as part of your listing presentation or as a handout after listing.*

Marketing Plan for [*Home*]

[*Date*]

_____

_____

_____

Dear _____ :

I would like to share with you our marketing plan for your home.

- Install sign [*and talking sign*].

- Take photographs of your home.

- Give you suggestions to help increase the marketability of your home.

- Prepare a property brief with a photo of your home emphasizing the desirable characteristics of the property.

- Install a lockbox on the property to aid in showing your home to prospective buyers.

- Enter your home in our multiple-listing service so the details of your property will be available to [_____] real estate offices and over [_____] salespeople.

- Send property briefs to other agents active in the area as well as discuss with them the benefits your home has to offer.

- Leave a supply of property briefs at your home for open house visitors and agent showings.

- Prepare a minimum of three separate classified ads for your home.

- Schedule ad placement.

- Meet with you to discuss ways that you can help in the marketing of your home.

- Prepare for and conduct [*our office agent visitation, and*] board visitation by real estate agents.

- Discuss your home with agents who visited it to find ways to enhance its marketability.

- Office agents will call all likely prospects they are currently working with about your home.

- Send direct mailings to area neighbors, followed by a telephone call, to enlist help in selecting a new neighbor.

- Prepare for and conduct an Open House.

- Follow up on all leads generated by calls about or visits to your home.

- Make weekly calls to all agents who used the lockbox about the interest of their buyers.

- Communicate weekly with you on our efforts and progress with your home as well as changes in the area market.

- Advertise your home along with other homes in your area and in the same price range, as well as continue our program of institutional advertising.

- Continue to make our best efforts to locate a buyer as well as internally evaluate those efforts until we are successful.

If you have any questions about this marketing plan outline, please call me.

Yours truly,

_____

Enclosure: [*Card*]

NOTE: *By keeping the simple heading Marketing Plan for [Home] and by deleting the first sentence, you could use this as an attachment to a letter to an owner thanking him or her for the listing (see pages 69 through 71).*

Seller's Net Proceeds Estimate Transmittal

[*Date*]

_____

_____

_____

Dear _____ :

Enclosed is a seller's net proceeds worksheet I have prepared for your property at [_____].

The net reflects [*your present mortgage being paid off and a sale at the list price of $ _____*].

I believe the figures on the worksheet are reliable, but they are estimates only and are not guaranteed.

If you have any questions, please call me.

Yours truly,

_____

Enclosures: [*Card, Seller Net Proceeds Estimate Worksheet*]

Seller Net Proceeds Estimate Worksheet

Estimated Seller's Net

Credits		Debits	
Sale price	$ _____	Loans being	
Impound account		assumed	$ _____
balance	_____	Other	
Prepaid		encumbrances	$ _____
insurance	_____	Loan prepayment	
Prepaid taxes	_____	penalties	$ _____
Other credits	_____	Agent fees	$ _____
Total		Escrow/attorney	$ _____
credits	$ _____	Abstract/title	
		insurance	$ _____
		Transfer tax	$ _____
		Termite	
		inspection	$ _____
		Real estate	
		taxes	$ _____
		Unpaid	
		assessments	$ _____
		Home protection	
		plan	$ _____
		Other	$ _____
		Total debits	$ _____

Total credits $ _____
Total debits $ _____
Seller net $ _____

NOTE: *Seller net would be cash and/or carryback financing in which the seller is financing the buyer.*

Agent Property Evaluation Transmittal Letter

[*Date*]

_____

_____

_____

Dear _____ :

Enclosed are copies of agent property evaluations made by agents at
our [*office caravan (and the) / multiple-listing service caravan*] on
[*give date(s)*]. The evaluations can provide valuable information
about your home.

I will be contacting you in the next few days to discuss these evaluations.

Yours truly,

_____

Enclosures: [*Agent property evaluations*]

Agent Property Evaluation

Property Address: _____   Date: _____
Name of Owner(s):   _____

   1. Feature of the home that will be most appeal-
       ing to buyers: _____
       _____
       _____
       _____

   2. Features or lack of features that buyers are
       likely to view as a negative: _____
       _____
       _____
       _____

   3. I feel that the price is
       too high _____   too low _____   realistic _____
       By how much? $ _____
       Why? _____
       _____

   4. To increase salability, the owner should con-
       sider: _____
       _____
       _____
       _____

NOTE: *Give this form to agents who view the home at office or MLS
caravans as well as those who attend an agent Open House.
Give the completed form to the owner.*

Ad Copy Transmittal

[*Date*]

_____

_____

_____

Dear _____ :

Enclosed is a copy of a classified advertisement, which appeared in the [_____] on [_____].

I am certain that you realize we receive many inquiries from our institutional advertising as well as from ads for specific property. What you may not be aware of is that few buyers actually end up purchasing the home they originally inquired about. After qualifying a buyer's needs and financial standing, we frequently find that the property in question does not fit the particular buyer. The buyer is then shown a number of other properties. In this way, every ad we place within a general price range serves as a sales tool for every home we have within that price range.

We will promote the sale of your home to the best of our ability. All of our advertisements benefit you, even those not specifically for your property. We have proven that our advertising methods work, and I feel confident they will be successful for your home.

Yours truly,

_____

Enclosures: [*Card, Ad copy*]

Progress Report

[*Date*]

_____

_____

_____

Dear _____ :

This note is to keep you informed of our efforts on your behalf. During the [*month / week*] of [_____], we

1. advertised your home in [*two newspapers*] using [*three*] ads with insertions on [*11*] days. (This is in addition to our institutional advertising and ads for other property in the same price range.)

2. have had more than [*50*] inquiries on your home and have had [*seven*] showings by our own salespeople.

3. have had [*five*] showings by salespeople from cooperating offices.

4. have had [*one*] open house and registered [*17*] guests.

5. have kept your home active in the Midvale Multiple-Listing Service available to [*107*] offices and more than [*1,000*] salespeople.

[*Although we have not yet received an offer on your home,*] we are very optimistic and will continue our efforts on your behalf.

Yours truly,

_____

Weekly Progress Report

[*Date*]

_____

_____

_____

Dear _____ :

The following weekly progress report describes our marketing efforts for your [*home*].

Week ending: [_____]

Property: [_____]

Owners: [_____]

Number of phone inquiries: [_____]

Number of showings: [_____]

Advertising: [_____

_____]

Electronic lockbox activity: [_____]

Open House

Date(s): [_____]

Number of visitors: [_____]

Comments of other agents and prospective buyers: _____

_____

_____

_____

_____

_____

If you have any questions, please contact me.

Yours truly,

_____

_____

Open House Results

[*Date*]

_____

_____

_____

Dear _____ :

This is just a short note to let you know about the open house we
held for your home on [*December 12th*].

We advertised the open house on [supply date(s)] in [supply news-
paper(s)] and set up [*directional signs / open house signs / and
flags*]. [*We also sent out letters to (neighbors) and (visitors to other
open houses).*]

I registered [*14*] visitors to the open house. [*Several additional visitors declined to register.*]

I will be contacting all the visitors to the open house within the next
few days to ascertain their needs as well as their interest in your
home.

[*The market is relatively slow right now; therefore, I think we need
to reexamine our strategy to excite buyers. I will call you in the next
few days to discuss ways in which we can increase the desirability
of your home.*]

[*I am very hopeful that, with our continued efforts, we will be able
to find that special buyer for your home.*]

Yours truly,

_____

_____

Change of Agents

[*Date*]

_____

_____

_____

Dear _____ :

[*Mr. Keith Swift*] of our office will be taking over the primary
responsibility of the sale of your home from [*Ms. Karen Jones*],
who is no longer with our office. [*Mr. Swift*] will call you in the next
few days to discuss our past and future efforts on your behalf.

If you have any questions at all, please do not hesitate to contact
either [*Mr. Swift*] or me. I have enclosed one of [*Mr. Swift's*] cards.

Yours truly,

_____

Enclosure: [*New agent's card*]

Price Adjustment Request—
New Comparative Market Analysis

[*Date*]

_____

_____

_____

Dear _____ :

Because of changes in the real estate marketplace, we have updated and enclosed the comparative market analysis of the value of your home.

From the sales figures of comparable homes recently sold, as well as from the asking prices of similar homes that remain unsold, you will see that homes priced above the present market value are not selling. You will also see the necessity for a price adjustment to conform to market conditions. After all, the marketplace ultimately determines at what price a property will sell.

I have enclosed a [*new listing / listing addendum*] reflecting the current real estate market. Please sign and return [*two*] copies to our office.

I will be calling you within the next few days to answer any questions that you might have.

Yours truly,

_____

Enclosures: [*Comparative market analysis, Listing addendum*]

NOTE: *It is better to blame the market rather than the home or the agency for the fact that a property has not sold. Never suggest "lowering" a price—the price is "adjusted" to reflect the market. Generally, a request to adjust a listing price should be made* in person *rather than by letter.*

Price Adjustment Request—
New Listing at Lower Price

[*Date*]

_____

_____

_____

Dear _____ :

The house at [_____] was recently listed for
[$ _____]. A copy of the [*listing / property flyer*] is
enclosed.

This home is [*only two blocks from your home / in an area as desirable as your home's area*] and is [*about the same size and age /
larger / newer*] than your home. Because of its price, it will tend to
make your home appear to be overpriced.

I don't want your home to be used as a comparison so that the other
home can be more readily sold. I will therefore be calling you in the
next few days to discuss pricing strategy.

Yours truly,

_____

Enclosure: [*Property flyer*]

NOTE: *This letter will make the owners realize that they are competing with other owners.*

Price Adjustment Request—
Lender Appraisal below List Price

[*Date*]

_____

_____

_____

Dear _____ :

I have just received the enclosed appraisal by [*Midvale Savings and Loan*] on your home.

Although I may not fully agree with this appraisal, it will nevertheless significantly affect prospective buyers, who will be reluctant to buy at a price above their lender's appraisal.

I therefore believe that it is in your best interest to adjust the price to reflect this appraisal. I have enclosed an addendum reflecting the new price. Please sign and return [*two*] copies.

[*If you have any questions, do not hesitate to call me. / I will be calling you in the next few days to answer any questions that you might have.*]

Yours truly,

_____

Enclosures: [*Appraisal report, Listing addendum*]

NOTE: Never *suggest "lowering" a price. The price is "adjusted" to reflect the lender's appraisal. Generally, any request to adjust a listing price should be made* in person *rather than by letter.*

Price Adjustment Request—Property Priced above Comparative Market Analysis

[*Date*]

_____

_____

_____

Dear _____ :

At the time we listed your home for sale at [*111 Midvale Drive*], our comparative market analysis indicated it had a market value of [*$125,500*]. Based on your decision as owner, the house was placed on the market at [*$150,500*].

Your home has now been on the market for [*90*] days. During this time we have advertised the property, called prospective buyers to discuss it, [*held an open house,*] and provided the listing information to a multiple-listing service available to [*93*] offices and [*1,141*] agents. Despite our best efforts, we have seen little interest in your home. Those who have seen it have expressed the opinion that your home, while desirable, is overpriced compared to other available properties.

Therefore, in our professional judgment the price should be adjusted to [*$125,500*], the figure indicated by our comparative market analysis. If you truly want to sell your home, I am certain that you will agree. I have enclosed a listing addendum that reflects this adjustment. Please sign and return [*two*] copies to my office.

I will be calling you in the next few days to answer any questions that you might have.

Yours truly,

_____

Enclosures: [*Listing addendum*]

Price Adjustment Request—
Based on Competition

[*Date*]

_____

_____

_____

Dear _____ :

I would like to bring you up-to-date on several recent events. The property at [*5 Crescent Lane*], which is very similar to your [*home*], has just been placed on the market at [*$* _____]. The property at [*532 Jupiter Avenue*], which was listed at [*$* _____], has just been sold for [*$* _____].

The market appears to be softening, which greatly reduces the likelihood of selling your home at the list price of [*$* _____]. If your home is to compete successfully in this market, I strongly suggest that the price be adjusted to [*$* _____]. I have included a listing addendum reflecting this adjustment. Please sign and return [*two*] copies to this office.

I will be calling you in a few days to answer any questions you might have.

Yours truly,

_____

Enclosure: [*Listing addendum*]

NOTE: *The letter creates a win-win situation. It does not criticize the property, which would result in a negative reaction; it places blame on the market. A "price adjustment" is requested rather than a price reduction; "reduction"* *would suggest the seller has to give something up. Since this list price was only an estimate of the sale price, a change in the list price is not a reduction. Nothing the owner had is being taken away.*

Make certain that you have both buyer's and seller's permission to give out information about completed transactions.

Price Adjustment Request—
Raise Price Based on Market Competition

[*Date*]

_____

_____

_____

Dear _____ :

Recent sales indicate that home prices are escalating. We have therefore prepared a new comparative market analysis for your home at [*111 Midvale Trail*].

You'll see that it indicates our current asking price is too low. While the low price would likely mean a very quick sale, we feel we can get you a higher price within a reasonable period of time.

I have included a listing addendum reflecting a price adjustment to [*$250,000*]. Please sign and return [*two*] copies to this office.

I will call you in a few days to answer any questions that you might have.

Yours truly,

_____

Enclosures: [*Comparative market analysis, Listing addendum*]

NOTE: *A letter is not the preferred method of asking for a price adjustment. A letter should be used only when personal contact cannot be made.*

Price Adjustment Request—Fixer-Upper

[*Date*]

_____

_____

_____

Dear _____ :

The current condition of your home at [*55 Lynn Court*] has made a sale difficult in our current market. As you know, [*the house needs decorating, the carpets need replacing and the home generally is showing the effects of its age*]. Unless you are willing to extensively rehabilitate the property, I would like your permission to advertise your home as a fixer-upper. This type of ad has strong appeal to many buyers who are not afraid of hard work and who meet these challenges with enthusiasm.

To attract this type of buyer, a price adjustment would be necessary. I suggest a price of [*$96,000*], and I have enclosed a listing addendum that reflects this adjusted price. Please sign and return [*two*] copies to this office.

I am confident that taking this approach will mean a timely sale of your property. I will be contacting you in the next few days to answer any questions that you might have.

Yours truly,

_____

Enclosure: [*Listing addendum*]

NOTE: *Again, the preferred method of communicating a request for a price adjustment is personal contact.*

Request for Minor Repairs

[Date]

_____

_____

_____

Dear _____ :

Several prospective buyers who have visited your home have com-
mented about the *[broken porch railing]*. Although this is not a
major problem, it nevertheless presents a significant negative image
to prospective buyers. We feel that it would be in your best interest
to arrange for the necessary repair as soon as possible.

*[Enclosed is a bid of ($ _____) to correct the problem(s). If
you will forward your check to me for this amount, I will authorize
the contractor to make the repairs.]*

I will call you in the next few days to answer any questions that you
might have.

Yours truly,

_____

Enclosures: *[Bid]*

Request for Minor Repairs—
Nonresident Owner

[*Date*]

_____

_____

_____

Dear _____ :

Your [*home*] at [———————————] needs some maintenance
work and repairs, including [_____
_____].

Enclosed is an estimate of [$ _____] for the necessary
work. If you will forward your check for this amount, we will see
that the work is accomplished. While the work suggested might
appear minor in nature, having your [*home*] in the best condition
possible will contribute to its salability as well as to the sales price.
When homes need work, buyers tend to believe that the owner is
desperate, and they are likely to reduce any offer they might otherwise make.

I will be calling you in the next few days to answer any questions
that you might have.

I look forward to placing a "Sold" sign in front of your [*home*].

Yours truly,

_____

Enclosures: [*Estimate*]

Request for Listing Extension

[*Date*]

_____

_____

_____

Dear _____ :

The activity concerning your home has increased, and I feel certain we will be successful in arranging a sale. We have been making our utmost efforts on your behalf because we realize how important a sale is to you. During the last [*six*] months, we have placed numerous advertisements, held open houses and provided information on your home to over [*39*] offices and [*900*] salespeople.

We want to continue our efforts until we are successful. I have enclosed an extension to our agency agreement. Please sign and return [*two*] copies immediately so we can continue our efforts to consummate a sale without interruption. I will be contacting you in the next few days to answer any questions you might have and to discuss a marketing plan that will mean a successful sale.

Yours truly,

_____

Enclosure: [*Agency agreement extension*]

NOTE: *Ideally, a request for a listing extension should be made* in *person. It is easier to say no to a letter than it is to a person.*

The words "agency agreement" are more positive than "listing." "Agency" implies a benefit while "listing" implies payment of a fee.

Listing Extended—Thank You

[*Date*]

_____

_____

_____

Dear _____ :

I would like to thank you personally for the confidence you have shown in [*Clyde Realty*] by extending our agency agreement on your [*home*] at [_____].

I want you to know that we are making our utmost efforts to locate a buyer. We realize how much a sale means to you. I feel certain that we will succeed in our quest for a buyer.

[*Enclosed is an executed copy of the agency agreement extension.*]

Yours truly,

_____

Enclosure: [*Agency agreement extension*]

Listing Expired—Thank You for Listing

[*Date*]

_____

_____

_____

Dear _____ :

I am very sorry you have decided not to renew our agency agreement. However, I want to thank you for having given [*Clyde Realty*] the opportunity to serve as your sales agent.

[*The market conditions were not favorable for a sale at the list price, although market conditions are now showing an improvement. / I feel a listing extension would result in a sale. However, with the present market, I recommend that you ask no more than ($ _____) for your home.*]

If you change your mind and wish to use the services of [*Clyde Realty*] again, I have enclosed a new agency agreement. By signing and returning [*two*] copies to our office, you will once again be certain that we will use our best efforts to serve your interests. [*The new agency agreement reflects our recommendations.*]

[*I will be calling you in the next few days to discuss some additional ideas that should help in marketing your home.*]

Yours truly,

_____

Enclosure: [*Agency agreement*]

Purchase Offer Transmittal #1

[*Date*]

_____

_____

_____

Dear _____ :

It took a lot of effort, but we were successful in obtaining the enclosed offer on your [*home*]. I believe it to be a reasonable offer, since it provides you with [*93%*] of the offering price.

If you agree with me, please sign and return the enclosed copies in the postage-paid envelope immediately. The buyers are not legally bound to this purchase until they receive a signed acceptance. Until that time, they have the right to cancel this offer.

I will be calling you to answer any questions that you might have.

Yours truly,

_____

Enclosure: [*Offer to purchase*]

NOTE: *Showing the offer as a percentage of the offering price tends to minimize the difference. Using the term "offering price" reminds the owner that this price is not sacred but is merely a hoped-for price.*

You create a sense of urgency by correctly pointing out that a buyer can back out prior to acceptance. Although sellers may refuse low offers, they don't like to allow the buyer to back out once an offer is made.

Whenever possible, offers should be presented in person. Letter presentations should be made only when face-to-face presentation is not practical.

Purchase Offer Transmittal #2

[*Date*]

_____

_____

_____

Dear _____ :

I told you that we would find a buyer, and I am now proud to present you with the enclosed offer. Although it is not everything we desired, because of market conditions, I believe that you will agree it is an exceptionally good sale.

Please sign and return [*two*] copies to me at once. As soon as I can notify the buyers of your acceptance, they will become legally bound to their purchase. Before the buyers are notified, they still have the right to revoke their offer. I will be calling you to answer any questions that you may have, or if you wish, call me [*collect*] as soon as you receive this offer.

Yours truly,

_____

Enclosure: [*Offer to purchase*]

Purchase Offer Transmittal #3

[*Date*]

_____

_____

_____

Dear —————— :

I am proud to enclose a [*full-price*] purchase offer from [*Janet Smith*]. [*The only deviation from your requirement is that Ms. Smith has requested a 60-day closing period.*]

Before she is notified of your acceptance, [*Ms. Smith*] could conceivably revoke her offer; therefore, please sign and return [*two*] copies in the enclosed, stamped envelope at once.

[*You may fax the acceptance copy to me at (give fax number); however, please mail the originals as directed.*]

Yours truly,

_____

Enclosure: [*Offer to purchase*]

_____

NOTE: *Call the owners as soon as they will have received the offer and express urgency.*

You will increase the percentage of acceptance for mailed offers if you send them by an overnight delivery service. It shows that you place great value on the offer.

Low Purchase Offer Transmittal

[*Date*]

_____

_____

_____

Dear _____ :

I have enclosed an offer we have received on your property at [*give address*]. The offer is not what we had hoped it would be. You now have three options:

1. Accept it. This would form a binding contract, and your home would be sold.

2. Reject it outright. This would end the negotiation process.

3. Make a counteroffer. You should realize that once a counteroffer is made, you can no longer accept the earlier offer, since that offer is considered to be dead. The buyers then have the option of accepting or rejecting your counteroffer.

If you feel you can't risk losing this buyer, I would recommend accepting the offer rather than making a counteroffer. If you can take the risk, I would recommend a counteroffer of [*$* _____], based on current market conditions, although the amount of the counteroffer is your decision.

Besides the acceptance, which can be enacted by your signature, I have also prepared a counteroffer reflecting my recommendations. Please sign and return [*two*] copies of whichever set of forms you decide to use.

I will be calling you in the next day or two to answer any questions you may have and to further discuss your options.

Yours truly,

_____

Enclosures: [*Offer to purchase, Counteroffer*]

Poor Offer Transmittal

[*Date*]

_____

_____

_____

Dear _____ :

As your agent, I am required to submit every offer received. I am therefore transmitting the enclosed purchase offer.

I recommend that you reject the offer as being unreasonable [*and make a counteroffer for* [$ _____], *which is enclosed for your signature.* / *and refrain from making any counteroffer*].

Although you have the right to accept the offer and form a binding contract, I hope that you will follow my advice; I do not think an acceptance would be in your best interest.

I will be calling you to answer any questions you may have, or if you like, call me collect at [_____].

Yours truly,

_____

Enclosure: [*Offer to purchase, Counteroffer*]

NOTE: *If the offer revealed specific problems, such as dangerous clauses like subordination agreements, or if the offer involved unsecured notes or trades of property having questionable value, you should specifically point out these problems.*

Seller Net Proceeds Estimate—After Offer

[*Date*]

_____

_____

_____

Dear _____ :

Enclosed is a seller net proceeds worksheet that I have prepared for your property, based on the buyer's offer of [$ _____].

I believe these figures are reliable but they are not guaranteed.

If you have any questions, please call me.

Yours truly,

_____

Enclosure: [*Seller Net Proceeds Worksheet*]

_____

NOTE: See page 82 for enclosure.

Offer Rejected

[*Date*]

_____

_____

_____

Dear _____ :

I'm very sorry the offer we received on your [*home*] failed to meet your expectations. As your agents, we have a duty to present every offer received.

I want you to know that we will continue with our best efforts to sell your [*home*], and we remain hopeful of an early success.

Yours truly,

_____

Information Letter—Status of Sale

[*Date*]

_____

_____

_____

Dear _____ :

[*The financing has been approved*] for [*Janet Jones / the Jones's / the purchaser(s)*] of your [*home*].

I will be contacting you within a few days to give you closing information.

Yours truly,

_____

Removal of Contingency

[*Date*]

_____

_____

_____

Dear _____ :

I am writing to notify you that [*The Jones's*] have signed the enclosed contingency release. Their purchase agreement now stands without the contingency of [*obtaining an* $8\frac{1}{2}$ *percent loan for 80 percent of the purchase price*].

[*We should be able to close the sale by* (give date).]

Yours truly,

_____

Enclosure: [*Contingency release*]

Failure of Buyer Contingency

[*Date*]

_____

_____

_____

Dear _____ :

As I said in our phone conversation, [*Mr. and Mrs. Smith*] have been unable to [*obtain financing*] according to the contingency set forth in their purchase offer.

Please sign the enclosed release forms so that I can return their deposit in accord with our agreement.

We have resumed our sales efforts and are confident of success in selling your home.

Yours truly,

_____

Enclosure: [*Release form*]

NOTE: *When it appears a contingency will not be met, inform the owner immediately so that failure will not come as a shock. Be certain that the seller agrees to the return of the deposit before it is returned. Otherwise, a court could later decide that the failure to meet the contingency was the fault of the buyer. If this is the case, you could be held liable for the returned deposit.*

For a release, use either a standard form or have an attorney prepare one for you.

Closing Documents Transmittal—
To Buyer or Seller

[*Date*]

_____

_____

_____

Dear _____ :

Enclosed are the following documents for [*your signature / both of your signatures*]: _____

_____

_____

_____

Please sign where indicated.

[*Important:* _____

_____

and _____

must be signed (in the presence of a notary public).]

Please return the documents as indicated by [*give date*].

Yours truly,

_____

Enclosures: [*Closing statement, Deed, Mortgage*]

Closing Status—To Buyer or Seller

[*Date*]

_____

_____

_____

Dear _____ :

[*The closing of your (home sale / home purchase) (should be on schedule). We expect to close on* (supply date).]

[*The closing of your (home sale / home purchase) may be delayed because* _____
_____ *I will inform you as soon as this is resolved.*]

[*We do not anticipate any problems with the closing. / If we encounter any problems, we will notify you immediately.*]

If you have any questions, please contact me.

Yours truly,

_____

_____

Notice of Closing

[*Date*]

_____

_____

_____

Dear _____ :

The closing for the sale of your home at [give address] will take place at [*our office at 9 AM*] on [*August 6*]. [*The seller must be present.*] The following checklist may be helpful to you:

Seller's Checklist

- ☐ Notify the post office of your change of address.
- ☐ Notify magazines, credit card companies, friends, and so on, of your address change.
- ☐ Cancel subscriptions to newspapers, or let them know of your change of address.
- ☐ Cancel service contracts such as pest control, gardener or water softener company.
- ☐ Cancel or transfer any homeowner's insurance coverage as of closing date.
- ☐ Disconnect or transfer utilities.
    - ☐ Water
    - ☐ Gas
    - ☐ Electricity
    - ☐ Phone
    - ☐ Cable TV
    - ☐ Trash
- ☐ Leave all warranties and manuals for appliances.

☐ Leave extra keys.

☐ Leave garage door openers.

If you have any questions concerning the closing, please contact me.

Yours truly,

_____

_____

Settlement Statement Transmittal

[*Date*]

_____

_____

_____

Dear _____ :

Enclosed is your check for [$ _____] as well as your settlement statement for the sale of your property at [*77 Lynn Court*].

We hope to be able to serve you for any future real estate needs.

Yours truly,

_____

Enclosures: [*Check, Settlement statement*]

NOTE: *Whenever possible, present checks in person. This gives you several opportunities: You can discuss an owner's future plans, ask for referrals, and request a testimonial letter.*

Closing Statement Question—To Buyer or Seller

[*Date*]

_____

_____

_____

Dear _____ :

In regard to your [*letter of* (give date) / *telephone call on (give date)*], I have reviewed your closing statement for [*give address*].

[*You are absolutely correct that an error was made, and I apologize for not discovering it. (I have enclosed a corrected statement and a check for $ _____ . / The escrow office will be sending you a corrected closing statement and a check).*]

[*The document preparation charge was for preparation of the Warranty Deed and the second mortgage and note. The charge of ($ _____) is a reasonable charge for this service in today's economy.*]

[*The charge for title insurance is based on Paragraph 16 of the Purchase Contract whereby you agreed to provide this policy. It is also normal for the seller to pay for a standard policy of title insurance and the buyer to pay for any extended coverage desired.*]

[*I will be calling you in the next few days to make certain that you fully understand the closing statement and to answer any other questions that you might have.*]

[*If you have any further questions or if I can be of service to you in any way, please do not hesitate to contact me.*]

Sincerely,

_____

Request for Return of Personal Property

[*Date*]

_____

_____

_____

Dear _____ :

The [*Smiths*] are now in their new home and are delighted with it. [*You certainly took excellent care of this fine home.*]

We do have a minor problem: The [*dining room ceiling fan*] was not in the house when the [*Smiths*] took possession. Your movers might have inadvertently packed it. As you realize, [*the purchase contract called for the ceiling fan to stay / the listing made a positive point of the ceiling fan remaining / the ceiling fan is regarded as a fixture, which must be left with the house unless agreed otherwise*].

Please pack and return the [*ceiling fan*] to the [*Smiths*] as soon as practical. Thank you in advance for your prompt attention to this matter.

Yours truly,

_____

cc: [*Smiths*]

NOTE: *This is a diplomatic letter asking for the return of an item.*

Notice to Builder of Defect

[*Date*]

_____

_____

_____

Dear _____ :

[*Mr. and Mrs. Riley*], who purchased your [*Glenway*] home at [give address] through our office, have informed us that [*the roof leaks in five places*]. They are very concerned about this matter. It would be greatly appreciated if this deficiency were promptly corrected. Small matters often become major problems if not taken care of quickly. More important, an unhappy buyer can detract from both of our reputations.

I look forward to continued beneficial cooperation between our firms and continued success in selling your homes.

Yours truly,

_____

cc: [*Mr. and Mrs. Riley*]

NOTE: *This letter sells the benefits of solving the problem.*

After-Closing Thank-You—To Buyer or Seller

[*Date*]

_____

_____

_____

Dear _____ :

I would like to thank you for letting me serve you in the [*sale of / purchase of*] your home. [*I am certain your new home will bring your family much happiness. / Based on the current market, I believe that the (sale / purchase) was very advantageous.*]

If I can be of any service to you in meeting your future real estate needs, do not hesitate to contact me. If you are happy with my services, I hope that you will recommend me to your friends.

Best wishes,

_____

_____

Service Evaluation—To Seller after Sale

[*Date*]

_____

_____

_____

Dear _____ :

To improve our service to sellers, we would appreciate very much if you would rate the services of [*Clyde Realty*] in the sale of your home.

Seller Evaluation of [*Clyde Realty*]

1. Do you feel that the listing agent understood your needs and concerns? ☐ Yes ☐ No

2. Do you feel that the listing agent accurately described the services we would provide? ☐ Yes ☐ No

3. Do you feel that the listing agent was realistic in his or her recommendations for listing price? ☐ Yes ☐ No

4. Did the listing agent make recommendations to you about the property, showings and open houses to increase the likelihood of a sale? ☐ Yes ☐ No

5. Do you feel that you were kept adequately informed about our efforts on your behalf as well as about what was happening in the market? ☐ Yes ☐ No

6. Do you feel that the agent was fair and honest in presenting the offer and in recommendations made? ☐ Yes ☐ No

7. During the time period between acceptance of the purchase offer and the closing, do you feel that you were kept adequately informed as to what was happening? ☐ Yes ☐ No

8. Would you recommend our firm to a friend who needed to sell his or her home? ☐ Yes ☐ No

9. Can we use your name as a satisfied seller or allow other owners to see your evaluation of [*Clyde Realty*]?

         ☐   Yes   ☐   No

10. Do you have any suggestions on how we can improve our service?   ☐   Yes   ☐   No

Please return this evaluation in the enclosed stamped envelope. Thank you for your time and consideration.

Yours truly,

⎡ *John Jones*   ⎤
⎣ *Broker, Clyde Realty* ⎦

NOTE: *Negative responses identify weaknesses so that greater effort can be expended in the future. Positive responses provide you with an excellent listing tool.*

Buyer or Seller Request for Testimonial Letter

[*Date*]

_____

_____

_____

Dear _____ :

[*I am glad that we were able to find a satisfactory buyer for your home and that we had no closing problems.*]

[*I am glad that we were able to be of service to you in finding a new home for your family.*]

Many people regard real estate salespeople as a necessary evil rather than as professionals who work to meet the needs of [*sellers / buyers*].

Because of this perception, I would appreciate if you could send me a brief letter describing the benefits you derived from the service I provided.

Testimonial letters from satisfied clients like you are effective in convincing others that it is in their best interest to work with a [*real estate professional* / REALTOR®] in [*selling / buying*] real estate.

Thank you in advance,

_____

Thank You for Testimonial Letter

[*Date*]

_____

_____

_____

Dear _____ :

I would like to thank you for your delightful letter of appreciation for my services. [*My (wife) / (husband), says that kind of praise will make me impossible to live with.*]

Your letter makes me proud to be regarded as one of the good [*guys / gals*] working to help others.

I will do my best to live up to the image you have given me in meeting any future real estate needs you might have. I want you to know that I am honored to have helped you in [*buying / selling*] your home.

All the best,

_____

Thank You For Your Trust

[*Date*]

_____

_____

_____

Dear _____ :

Just a note to say "Thank you" for [*entrusting the sale of your home to me / allowing me to help you buy your new home*].

All too often in today's rush of doing business, we forget to say "Thanks." But not this time.

I have enjoyed fulfilling your needs. If I can do anything else for you, please call on me.

Sincerely,

_____

_____

Notification to Seller of Referral

[Date]

_____
_____
_____

Dear _____ :

I am delighted that we were able to find a buyer for your home, but I am sad you will be leaving our community. One of the problems in real estate sales is that you really get to like people and then they are gone. However, I wish you great happiness in *[Richmond]*.

To help you meet your housing needs, I have contacted *[Tom Smith]* of *[Smith Realty]* in *[Richmond]*. *[Tom]* will be calling you in a few days to go over your special housing needs. *[He]* can arrange for you to check out a group of homes when you arrive. *[Both our offices and (Smith Realty) are members of (Worldwide Referrals). It is a cooperative organization of over (1,800) real estate professionals concerned with meeting the relocation needs of homeowners.]* I have also contacted the *[Richmond]* Chamber of Commerce, and they will be sending you area information and maps.

If I can ever be of service to you again, please don't hesitate to contact me.

Your friend,

_____

_____

Chapter

6

Owner Cancellation / Breach of Listing

Release of Listing

[Date]

_____

_____

_____

Dear _____ :

You have indicated *[by your letter of April 3]* that you no longer wish *[Clyde Realty]* to represent you in the sale of *[your home]* at *[2137 Northbridge Road]*.

Therefore, I have enclosed a release form that releases you and *[Clyde Realty]* from any and all obligations under *[the Exclusive Right-to-Sell Listing dated March 1, 1994]*, and cancels said listing agreement.

Please sign two copies of the enclosed release *[where indicated]* and return them to me in the enclosed stamped envelope. I will then sign them and return a copy to you.

I am sorry that we were unable to meet your needs. Please call me if you have any questions.

Yours truly,

_____

_____

Enclosures: *[Release]*

NOTE: Use a listing release form either prepared by your attorney or one endorsed by your local professional real estate organization. Do not attempt to draft your own legal document.

Demand for Commission—
Owner Removes Property from Market

[*Date*]

_____

_____

_____

Dear _____ :

In accord with an exclusive agency contract dated [_____],
[*Clyde Realty*] has been diligent in searching for a buyer for your
property at [_____].

On [give date], before the expiration of the agency contract, you
[*informed this office that the property was no longer available for
sale*]. Under the terms of the contract, demand is hereby made for
[$ _____], which is [*6 percent of the list price, the amount
specified as damages if you remove the property from the market or
otherwise make it unmarketable prior to the expiration of our
agency agreement*].

If you have any questions, please contact me by [give date].

Yours truly,

_____

_____

NOTE: *Giving a deadline increases the likelihood of an owner
response.*

Response to Owner or Attorney— Cancellation of Listing

[Date]

_____

_____

_____

Dear _____ :

I have received your letter of [give date] in which you unilaterally cancel the listing agreement of [give date] on the property located at [_____].

[We have worked diligently toward the sale of said property and have been meeting our contractual obligations. Therefore, under the terms of the listing, demand is hereby made for ($ _____) as commission owed based on the breach of the contract in canceling the exclusive right-to-sell agency agreement].

[Although we have worked diligently toward the sale of the property, we do understand the unique circumstances involved and are willing to meet with you in the hope of reaching a mutually satisfactory settlement].

[If you have any questions, please contact me by (give date).]

Yours truly,

_____

Owner Removes Property from Market

[*Date*]

_____

_____

_____

Dear _____ :

By your request, we will no longer advertise or show your [*home*] at [give address] for sale. We will also take down our sign and remove the property from our multiple-listing service.

The listing, as agreed, will remain in full force and effect. If you or anyone else sells the [*house*] while our agreement is in effect, we will of course expect our full compensation under the terms of our exclusive right-to-sell listing.

If you later decide to sell your home, we hope that you will consider the services and courtesy we have shown you.

Yours truly,

_____

_____

NOTE: *This is not a release. A release from the listing would allow the owner to sell without paying any commission. This offers you protection if the owner asks to be released with the intention of avoiding commission payment because he or she has secretly located a buyer.*

Demand for Commission—
Owner's Action Prevents Sale

[*Date*]

_____

_____

_____

Dear _____ :

Pursuant to our [*exclusive agency listing agreement*] for your property at [_____], our office was successful in obtaining an offer on said property. You accepted this offer to purchase on [give date].

A sale was not concluded because you [*were unable to clear title / failed to comply with the condition that the roof be replaced / refused to complete the transaction*].

Since our office has fully complied with the terms of said listing agreement in obtaining a buyer who was ready, willing and able to buy under the price and terms you agreed to, demand is hereby made for a commission of [$ _____] based on the purchase price of [$ _____].

If you have any questions, please contact me by [give date].

Yours truly,

_____

_____

NOTE: *Before sending this letter, check with your own attorney. The deadline to contact you provides a hint of dire consequences if the owner fails to do so.*

Demand for Commission—
Owner Refuses Full-Price Offer

[*Date*]

_____

_____

_____

Dear _____ :

Under the terms of our exclusive listing agreement dated
[_____], [*Clyde Realty*] worked diligently to obtain a
buyer for your property at [_____].

On [*August 1, 1990*], we presented you with a full-price offer of
[$ _____] in full accord with the terms specified in the list-
ing agreement. The buyer, [*Jane Jones*], was ready, willing and able
to complete the purchase.

You responded to said offer by [*refusing to sell / countering the
offer with a price greater than the listing price / demanding cash
when the listing agreement provided for you to carry back a
$50,000 second mortgage*].

Because the sale was prevented by your refusal to sell under the
terms of our agency agreement, demand is hereby made for a commission of [$ _____] in accordance with paragraph [*six*] of
said agreement.

If you have any questions, please contact me by [*August 15*].

Yours truly,

_____

_____

NOTE: *By setting a deadline, you force the recipients to consider
their options. While a letter puts the demand on record, you
should make personal contact to try to resolve the problem.*

Chapter

7

Residential Buyer Solicitation

Warning: It is a violation of federal law to direct buyers toward or away from a neighborhood based on race, sex, ancestry, religion, handicap or familial status.

Letter to Neighbor after Listing

[*Date*]

_____

_____

_____

Dear _____ :

Our office has recently listed the home of your neighbor [*John Jones*] at [*322 Maple Lane*] for sale. You have probably noticed our "For Sale" sign.

I am writing you to ask for your help in locating a buyer for this fine home. In other words, I want you to think about helping to choose your new neighbor.

The home has [*three bedrooms, two baths and a den*] [*and, as you know, it has been lovingly cared for*]. It is priced much lower than you would think, so anyone you suggest would be thankful for your recommendation. I will be calling you in a few days to see if you can suggest any friends or acquaintances who might want to be your neighbor.

Sincerely,

_____

_____

Enclosure: [*Card*]

NOTE: *Be certain to follow through by calling the neighbors.*

Tired of Renting?

[*Date*]

_____

_____

_____

Dear _____ :

Tired of Renting?

- Would you like to enjoy the privacy of your own home?
- Would you like affordable home payments?
- Would you like home equity rather than rent receipts?

Do you want to find out how you can be an owner rather than a renter with a down payment and monthly payments tailored to your individual needs?

I will be calling you in the next few days to explain how you can become a homeowner NOW!

Yours truly,

_____

Enclosure: [*Card*]

NOTE: *This letter, as well as others in this section, are directed toward turning tenants into owners. For mailings, we suggest using a reverse directory to target apartment dwellers. Letters to units that have many younger families will be especially productive.*

Escape the Landlord

[*Date*]

_____

_____

_____

Dear _____ :

Want to

Escape the Landlord?

If you're tired of collecting rent receipts and would like to have something for your money, I have homes for you:

- Very low or even no down payment
- Monthly payments similar to rent
- Three and even four bedrooms
- Your own [*double*] garage
- Your own [*fenced*] backyard

I will call you in a few days to show you how easy it can be to escape your landlord.

Yours truly,

_____

Enclosure: [*Card*]

Love Your Landlord?

[*Date*]
_____
_____
_____

Dear _____ :

Do you

Love Your Landlord?

I bet your landlord loves you. Your landlord gets the rent and tax deductions, and you get rent receipts. That's a pretty good deal—for your landlord.

Kiss Your Landlord Good-bye

A low-low-down payment or even a no-down payment loan can put you in your own home by [*Easter*]. I will be calling you in the next few days to get you started toward becoming your own landlord.

Yours truly,

_____

Enclosure: [*Card*]

Offer To Qualify for a Loan

[*Date*]

_____

_____

_____

Dear _____ :

Can You Afford To Buy a Home?

With low interest rates and many motivated sellers, chances are that you can not only become a homeowner, but you may likely qualify for a much finer home than you believed possible.

Free Loan Qualifying Analysis

I will call you in the next few days to arrange to obtain some very basic information that will allow me to prepare, at *no* cost or obligation to you, a homebuyer qualifying analysis. This [*computer-generated*] analysis will show you how to finance under a variety of available loans, including some having no down payments and very low down payments.

Yours truly,

_____

Enclosure: [*Card*]

NOTE: *This is an excellent approach for young families who are currently renters.*

Tenant Solicitation

[*Date*]

_____

_____

_____

Dear _____ :

Before we advertise to the general public, we would like to give you the first opportunity to purchase the home at [give address]. It has just been placed on the market.

I will be calling you in the next few days to provide any information you may desire and to discuss various possible financing arrangements.

Yours truly,

_____

Enclosure: [*Card*]

NOTE: *This letter gives very little information, but makes the tenant think of the possibility of becoming an owner and of your upcoming call.*

If the tenants do not plan to be the buyers for the home they are living in, they will either be buyers or tenants for another property.

Tenant Solicitation—Condominium Conversion

[*Date*]

_____

_____

_____

Dear _____ :

As you may be aware, [*John Jones*], the owner of your apartment building, [*is in the process of converting your building to condominiums / has received approval to convert your building's units to cooperatives*]. Our office will be handling the sale of the units.

As the tenant, you have the first opportunity to purchase your unit, which will be available for [*$187,500*]. If you are interested, I would like to show you the various financing options available. I will be contacting you in the next few days to discuss the advantages of ownership.

Yours truly,

_____

Enclosure: [*Card*]

NOTE: *The current tenants have three choices:*

    1. Buy the unit they currently occupy.

    2. Buy somewhere else.

    3. Find a new rental.

Offer To Aid in Tenant Relocation

[*Date*]

_____

_____

_____

Dear _____ :

I would like to offer my services to help you meet your relocation housing needs for rental or home purchase. I will call you in the next few days to tell you about low- and no-down payment home purchase opportunities, as well as what is available in the local rental market.

Yours truly,

_____

Enclosure: [*Card*]

NOTE: *This letter could be used when apartments are converted to cooperatives or condominiums, or when property is taken by eminent domain or razed for redevelopment.*

Marriage or Engagement

[*Date*]

_____

_____

_____

Dear _____ :

Congratulations on your recent [*marriage / engagement*]!

I would like to offer my assistance in meeting any present or future housing needs. We have rentals ranging from [$ _____] to [$ _____] a month and homes that can be purchased with down payments and financing tailored to your particular needs.

I will be calling you in the next few days to offer you housing consultation with no cost or obligation.

Yours truly,

_____

Enclosure: [*Card*]

New Parents

[*Date*]

_____

_____

_____

Dear _____ :

Congratulations on your new [*son / daughter*]!

Although I won't help out with the 2:00 AM feeding or the diapers, I can help you if you need more family space.

We have an unusually good selection of family homes, many of which offer flexible financing to meet individual buyers' needs.

I will call you in the next few days to show you how easy it can be to own your own single-family home with a [*child-safe, fenced*] backyard that is all yours.

Yours truly,

_____

Enclosure: [*Card*]

NOTE: *Birth announcements in newspapers are particularly effective for targeting addresses of families who are living in apartments, condominiums or mobile homes.*

Open House—Invitation to a Neighbor

[*Date*]

_____

_____

_____

Dear _____ :

I would like you to [*be my guest for coffee and cake / visit with me*] on

[*Sunday*] [*October 12th*]
[*1 – 4 PM*]

at the [*Johnson Residence / Former Johnson Residence*], [give address].

You will be able to view this fine home, which we are proud to offer for sale. Please bring any friends who might be interested in becoming your new neighbor. I look forward to seeing you!

Yours truly,

_____

Enclosure: [*Card*]

Open House—Invitation to Previous Visitor

[*Date*]

_____
_____
_____

Dear _____ :

You visited one of our open houses on [give date], at [give address] [*in Orchard Ridge*].

I want to tell you about [*several other / an*] open house[*s*] we will have [*this coming Saturday and Sunday*], [give date(s)], from [*11 AM to 4 PM*].

[*Addresses*]

_____

[*Basic features*]

_____

_____

[*Price*] _____

If you are interested in a new home, [*this is a / these are two*], [*home(s)*] you will definitely want to see. I think that you will be delighted with the area, the special features offered and the value.

[*Oh! Bring this letter with you and I will have (an LA Dodgers baseball cap) / (a special free gift) for you!*]

Yours truly,

_____

Enclosure: [*Card*]

_____

NOTE: *Letters such as this will increase open house traffic as well as show the owners that you are expending extra effort on their behalf. A free gift such as a baseball cap or a coffee mug with your firm's name on it will increase the effectiveness of the letter.*

Open House—Visitor Rating Form

Name: _____ Property:

_____

Address: _____

Phone: _____

Date: _____

Reason for visiting this open house: ☐ advertising
☐ signs   ☐ other (specify): _____

Features I particularly like: _____

_____

_____

Features I do not like: _____

_____

_____

_____

I believe the price quoted is: ☐ low   ☐ about right
                                 ☐ high

Do you presently own your home? _____

Is it currently for sale? _____

General comments: _____

_____

_____

NOTE: *This is a form rather than a letter. It is designed to obtain useful information for listing and selling. Of course, you should relay information concerning the property to the owner.*

Open House—Thank You to Visitor

[*Date*]

_____

_____

_____

Dear _____ :

I would like to thank you for visiting our firm's open house at [give address] [*last weekend*].

I will be calling you in the next few days to ask you your impression of the house and how it fits your needs. I have also enclosed information on several other available homes. If you are interested in any of them, I will be happy to arrange a showing.

Yours truly,

_____

Enclosures: [*Card, Property information*]

NOTE: *A letter saying you will call forces a person to think about the call and what they will tell you. It is a power approach to letter writing.*

Notice of Sale to Open House Visitor

[*Date*]

_____

_____

_____

Dear _____ :

The open house you recently viewed at [give address] has just been
sold. We have, however, recently received several very attractive
new listings that I feel will be of great interest to you.

I feel certain I can find the perfect home for you as to size, location,
price and terms. I will call you in the next few days to determine
your specific housing needs so that I can begin to work for you.

Yours truly,

_____

Enclosure: [*Card*]

Property Inquiry Letter #1

[*Date*]

_____

_____

_____

Dear _____ :

The [*111 Midvale Lane*] property that you have inquired about offers a very special opportunity. Although you really must see the property in person to fully appreciate it, I have enclosed a descriptive sheet for you.

I will be calling you in the next few days to answer any questions you may have and to tell you about several other properties that might be of interest to you.

Yours truly,

_____

Enclosures: [*Card, Property brief*]

_____

NOTE: *The purpose of the call would be to set up a definite time to show the property.*

Property Inquiry Letter #2

[*Date*]

_____

_____

_____

Dear _____ :

I am very happy to send you the material that you requested on the [*30 acres and 2 houses*] advertised in the [*Sunday Daily Ledger*].

I have also included information on several similar properties that are available. I will call you in a few days so we can arrange for you to view several rare opportunities.

Yours truly,

_____

Enclosures: [*Property briefs*]

Chamber of Commerce Inquiry

[*Date*]

_____

_____

_____

Dear _____ :

The [*Midvale*] Chamber of Commerce has indicated that you are considering becoming one of our neighbors.

Perhaps I am a bit premature, but I would like to welcome you to our community and offer you our relocation assistance. I would be happy to arrange motel reservations when you visit the area. If you desire any specific information, let me know.

Included is some general information about several of our housing opportunities. I have also enclosed a Housing Needs Checklist which will help me in meeting your specific needs. I will call you in the next few days to find out when I can show you our community and the many fine homes we are offering.

Yours truly,

_____

Enclosures: [*General area information, Housing Needs Checklist*]

NOTE: *See the Housing Needs Checklist on page* xx.

Person Contemplating Moving to the Area

[*Date*]

_____

_____

_____

Dear _____ :

[*XYZ, Inc.*] informed us that you may be moving to our community. I would like to offer my services to help you meet your housing needs.

I have included information on several of the properties currently available; however, if you would fill out the enclosed checklist, I will prepare housing information specific to your particular needs.

Yours truly,

_____

Enclosures: [*Property information, Housing Needs Checklist*]

NOTE: *Sources for information about people moving to your area could be the local chamber of commerce, local school districts, personnel offices of local firms, other agents, etc. When you send inquiries to these potential sources, include a postage-paid addressed envelope.*

If you do not receive a response within ten days, follow up the letter with a phone call.

Housing Needs Checklist

[*Clyde Realty*]
[*1320 West Main*]
[*Midvale, IL 60793*]
[*(321) 935-9090*]

Housing Needs Checklist

Presently I own a home _____ rent _____
I must sell before I relocate _____
My home is currently on the market _____
I prefer to rent _____ to purchase _____
I prefer a single-family home _____ condominium
_____ apartment _____
Estimated rental range: $_____ to $ _____

Estimated purchase price:

_____	Under $60,000
_____	$60,000-$80,000
_____	$80,000-$100,000
_____	$100,000-$125,000
_____	$125,000-$150,000
_____	$150,000-$200,000
_____	$200,000-$250,000
_____	Over $250,000

Size of family: _____
Names and ages of children: , _____ ;
_____ , _____ ; _____ ,
_____
Number of bedrooms desired: _____
Number of baths desired: _____
Particular locations I am interested in (if known): _____
_____
Required special features: _____
_____
Desired special features: _____
_____

I expect to be
     checking the area around _____
     relocating around [*give date*] _____

Name: _____
Address: _____
Phone: _____

NOTE: *This checklist can be used as an enclosure with the answer to any inquiry about property.*

The price range might need to be adjusted to reflect your local market.

Request for Buyer Information

[*Date*]

_____

_____

_____

Dear _____ :

To best meet your housing needs, I would appreciate if you could complete the enclosed Prospective Buyer Confidential Information form.

Although some of the questions may seem personal, we need this information to understand your needs and to prequalify you for any required loan. This is really the first step toward locating a new home for you and your family. Thank you!

Yours truly,

_____

Enclosures: [*Card, Prospective Buyer Confidential Information form*]

Prospective Buyer
Confidential Information Form

Prospective Buyer Confidential Information

Name(s): _____   Phone: _____

Address: _____

Size of family: _____

Names and ages of children or other dependents living with you: _____ , _____ ;

_____ , _____ ;

_____ , _____

Initial contact with this firm was motivated by (advertisement, sign, referral, etc.): _____

Present address: _____

How long at above address: _____

Do you presently own your own home? _____

If yes, must you sell before you buy? _____

If yes, is your present home currently listed for sale? _____ With: _____

How long has it been on the market? _____

Your reason(s) for seeking to buy a new home: _____

_____

_____

How long have you been looking for a new home? _____

Have you found any home that you like? _____
If yes, why didn't you purchase it? _____
Areas or locations that are of special interest to you: __
_____
_____
Why? _____
_____
_____
Do you currently own all of your own appliances (stove,
refrigerator, washer/dryer)? _____
What features do you like about your present home? __
_____
What features don't you like about your present home?
_____
_____
Why? _____
_____
_____
What are your hobbies or special interests? _____
_____
_____
Have you qualified for or been turned down for a home
loan within the past year? _____
If you qualified for a loan, what was the name of the firm
and loan amount? _____

Approximate monthly gross income (before taxes and other deductions): $ _____

Total monthly payments on long-term debt (one year or more revolving credit accounts plus car, etc.):
$ _____

What are you willing to invest toward a down payment on a home? $ _____

This form will be kept in a confidential prospective-buyer file by

[*Clyde Realty*]

[*Telephone*]

NOTE: *This form could be used as a mailing enclosure or could be delivered in person to determine housing needs and financial qualification.*

Chapter

8

Business and Investment Buyer Solicitation

Builder Solicitation—Lots

[*Date*]

_____

_____

_____

Dear _____ :

We have recently listed [*20*] lots in [*Midvale Heights*]. The lots all have [*sewer and water installed and paid for*], and they are competitively priced from [*$27,500 to $31,500, with terms possible*].

I will be calling you in the next few days to discuss a convenient time to show you these desirable building sites.

Yours truly,

_____

Enclosure: [*Card*]

NOTE: *The letter takes for granted the reader's interest, and the mention of a phone call forces the reader to spend a few seconds on the idea of lots in the area specified. The phone call should offer the choice of time of showing, not ask whether the builder wants a showing.*

Adjoining Owner Solicitation

[Date]

_____

_____

_____

Dear _____ :

I have just listed the property at [*111 Midvale Lane*] for sale. Since this property adjoins your property, we felt that you should have the first opportunity to purchase it. I am therefore notifying you before we advertise to the general public.

I am certain that you understand the advantage of owning this adjoining parcel. I will call you in the next few days to provide you with any specific information you might desire.

Yours truly,

_____

Enclosure: [*Card*]

NOTE: *This letter is a teaser. It creates urgency and a desire to know the price. This approach can be used for raw land, lots, farms and even income or investment property. A great many properties are sold to adjoining property owners.*

Owner of Similar Investment Property in Area

[*Date*]

_____

_____

_____

Dear _____ :

When we listed the [*24-unit apartment building at 3305-3307 Chestnut Boulevard*], I immediately thought that this would be the ideal investment for the owner of the property at [*3309 Chestnut Boulevard*].

Because the property [*is right next door to your property / is so close to your property and is so similar*], the management advantages of dual ownership are apparent.

The property is available at [*an attractive price with flexible terms / $1.5 million with approximately $150,000 down / a price and terms that will allow an immediate positive cash flow*]. I will be calling you in the next few days to discuss the advantages that this fine property can offer you.

Yours truly,

_____

P.S. If you are not interested in purchasing this property, perhaps you would consider selling your property. The advantages to a buyer owning both properties could make for an exceptional sale opportunity.

Enclosure: [*Card*]

NOTE: *The P.S. raises the point that if the readers aren't buyers, they should be sellers. It also reinforces the advantages of owning two similar properties.*

Tenant Solicitation of Ownership

[Date]

_____

_____

_____

Dear [Ms. Perkins*]:

How would you like your office to be in [Perkins* Plaza / the Perkins* Building] and not have to move?

Your present [office building / commercial building] has just been placed on the market. It offers you a rare opportunity. You can be your own landlord and be entitled to depreciation, income and appreciation instead of just a growing pile of rent receipts.

I will contact you in the next few days to show you how [Perkins* Plaza] can become a reality.

Yours truly,

_____

Enclosure: [Card]

*Use tenant's name here.

NOTE: _This letter should be sent to professional tenants and strong retail tenants. It has an excellent approach to pride by naming the building after the solicited buyer. A variation of this approach is to superimpose the tenant's name on an enclosed photo of the building._

Tenant Solicitation—Office Condominium

[*Date*]

_____

_____

_____

Dear _____ :

Do you realize that you could move your office less than [*3 blocks*] away and have

- Absolute protection against future rent increases
- The tax advantage of depreciation
- Payments that increase your equity rather than worthless rent receipts
- An investment that will likely show exceptional appreciation
- A hedge against inflation

I have [*several / an*] outstanding office condominium[*s*] for sale that offer[*s*] you advantages that a rental cannot provide, and are bound to please your accountant. I should be able to make you an owner with little or no increase in actual monthly costs and a down payment tailored to your needs.

This may sound too good to be true, but I will prove it to you and your accountant. You can avoid saying "I should have . . . " in the future by investigating now.

I will be calling you within the next few days to give you more information on this very special opportunity.

Yours truly,

_____

NOTE: *By canvassing the buildings close to your listing or by using a reverse directory, you can put together a sizable mailing list.*

Franchise—General Needs

[*Date*]

_____

_____

_____

Attention: Real Estate Officer

I would like to be your real estate eyes and ears in [*the Clark and Humboldt Counties*].

If you would let me know your real estate needs regarding size, traffic count, access, demographics, price or rent, and so on, I would be happy to put my area knowledge to work for you.

Yours truly,

_____

Enclosure: [*Card*]

NOTE: *Names and addresses of franchises are available from franchise magazines as well as from several books on franchises. The research librarian at your local public library can help you locate these resources.*

Franchise—Specific Location

[Date]

_____

_____

_____

Dear _____ :

Our office has recently listed [*a property at 55 Chestnut Boulevard /
the property in the enclosed flyer*]. Because of [*access and traffic*], I
feel that it would be an excellent location for one of your franchises.
The parcel is [*200 feet × 100 feet*]. An attractive [*purchase price /
lease*] is available. Please let me know if you are interested.

I am willing to work with you in meeting your real estate needs
within [*Dade County*]. If you could let me know your specific interests, my eyes, ears, and expertise are available for you.

Yours truly,

_____

Enclosure: [*Flyer, Card*]

NOTE: *Names and addresses of franchises are available from franchise magazines as well as from several books on franchises. The research librarian at your local public library
can help you locate these resources.*

White Elephant Investment

[*Date*]

_____

_____

_____

Dear _____ :

Do you know

What To Do with a White Elephant?

We are looking for an investor with vision who can create a productive use for [*a seven-story, 74,000-square-foot, former textile plant with rail siding on a three-acre site north of Highway 30.*]

Although it's a problem, the price of [*$690,000*] reflects that. If you have a solution, someone else's problem can be your opportunity.

I will call you in the next few days to arrange a private showing and perhaps we can brainstorm a solution to the problem.

Yours truly,

_____

_____

NOTE: *This is an excellent letter for owners of property in the area, creative investors, and developers. A letter such as this intrigues investors and speculators. It is an excellent way to gain initial personal access to major buyers of investment property.*

Safe Investment—Net Lease

[*Date*]

_____

_____

_____

Dear _____ :

Do you

Want [*a Great Investment?*]

Would you like monotonous rent checks, month after month, year after year [*while the tenant pays the taxes and makes the repairs*]?

If a carefree investment guaranteed by a financially strong tenant interests you and you can handle a [*$250,000*] down payment, then this could be the investment you have been waiting for.

I will be calling you in the next few days, if you don't call me first, to arrange a private showing of a very special opportunity.

Yours truly,

_____

Enclosure: [*Card*]

NOTE: *As written, this solicitation is for a triple-net property leased to a strong tenant.*

Mailings should be to investors owning larger quality properties as well as to doctors, attorneys and CPAS. A letter such as this allows you to expand the size and quality of your list of potential real estate investors.

$100,000 Investment

[*Date*]

_____

_____

_____

Dear _____ :

Want something

Better than a Jumbo CD?

I have a real estate investment that offers

- A financially strong tenant
- A hedge against inflation
- Leverage opportunities
- Possible appreciation
- Professional management

Plus, the income is better than the income you would get from CDs, and this income will be partially sheltered.

I will call you within the next few days to discuss the benefits offered by this extraordinary real estate investment.

Yours truly,

_____

Enclosure: [*Card*]

NOTE: *Income will be sheltered by depreciation. Jumbo certificates of deposit (CDs) come in $100,000 denominations. See note following prior letter.*

Referral Investor

[*Date*]

_____

_____

_____

Dear _____ :

[*Alice Smith*] recommended that I contact you. We have [*just listed / available*] an exceptional investment opportunity that [*she*] thought might interest you.

It is a [*low-risk*] property offering the [*possibility of extraordinary appreciation coupled with tax-sheltered income*]. It would require a down payment of around [*$110,000*].

I will be contacting you in the next few days to determine if this property would fulfill your investment needs.

Yours truly,

_____

NOTE: *This letter gives little detail other than amount of down payment. It is intended to get the recipients to consider owning investment property and to prepare them so you can qualify them according to their specific needs. Although you must have an actual property, the letter is used to tantalize. Providing more details would increase the likelihood that the recipient will interpret some of those details as negative.*

Syntax Formation

Syndicate Formation

[Date]

_____

_____

_____

Dear _____ :

I am putting together a small group of local investors [*to take part in an exceptional investment opportunity as limited partners / to take advantage of the exceptional opportunities available now in distressed income property.*] [*Joe Jones has recommended you as a person who would appreciate taking part in this opportunity. / You indicated some time ago that I should contact you if a really great opportunity presented itself.*]

Since you are knowledgeable in investment matters, you will understand the desirability of a prime, low-risk real estate investment [*at a bargain basement price*].

Investors must be able to make a [*$20,000*] minimum investment. I will call you in the next few days to determine your interest in attending an informal meeting of potential investors at my home at [*1744 Midvale Lane*] on [*Saturday morning, April 10th at 10 AM*]. After I have discussed the opportunity and answered any questions, those who are interested will have an opportunity to visit the property.

Yours truly,

_____

Enclosure: [*Card*]

NOTE: *A morning home meeting provides a nonthreatening atmosphere. Also, forming a group meeting tends to reduce apprehension. For a syndicate solicitation, be certain that you have checked your state laws. Syndicates may be subject to federal and state registration unless they fit into an exemption. Consult an attorney before you attempt to form a syndicate.*

Operating Income and Expenses

[*Date*]

_____

_____

_____

Dear _____ :

[*In accord with your request,*] the following is a statement of income and expenses for the property located at [_____]. The figures set forth are based on [*a copy of the latest tax return provided by the owner / a statement provided by the owner / the books provided to us by the owner / the property management statements / information furnished by the owner's accountant*].

Income

Scheduled gross annual income	$ _____
Vacancy and collection loss	($ _____)
Adjusted gross annual income	$ _____

Expenses

Taxes [*1993*]	$ _____
Insurance cost [*1993*]	$ _____
Policy provider [*Jones Underwriters*]	
Utilities [*based on last 12 months*]	$ _____
Management costs [*for last 12 months*]	$ _____
Maintenance and repairs [*1993*]	$ _____
Total expenses	($ _____)
[*(before debt service)*]	
Net operating income	$ _____
[*(not considering debt service)*]	

It should be pointed out that just a [*six*] percent annual increase in rents would increase the net income by [*$ _____*] within [*three*] years, and rentals have been experiencing an annual increase of [*over six*] percent a year. Most of this increase would be reflected in the net.

I will call you within the next few days to answer any questions you may have and to show you why I feel this investment opportunity deserves your immediate and serious consideration.

Yours truly,

_____

Enclosure: [*Card*]

NOTE: *Minor modification would turn this letter into an operating income and expense statement to be attached to* property briefs *(flyers describing properties).*

Of course, you must have an owner's permission to give out income and expense data.

Notice to Business Owner of
Related Business for Sale

[*Date*]

_____

_____

_____

Dear _____ :

Because you are in the [*retail hardware*] business, you now have an exceptional opportunity for expansion.

We have just listed for sale a [*successful hardware store*] that offers great potential. The books are open to you and your accountant. I will be calling you in a few days with more details. I believe that this opportunity deserves your immediate attention.

Yours truly,

_____

Enclosure: [*Card*]

NOTE: *This letter is a teaser to excite interest. The letter should give very little information about the business, and the letter should not identify the particular business being offered at this time.*

Keep in mind that financial information concerning a property or business should never be given out to anyone without the owner's permission.

Supplier or Wholesaler—Business Opportunity

[*Date*]

_____

_____

_____

Dear _____ :

Because you are a [*hardware distributor* / *hardware wholesaler*], I thought that you should be aware of the [*retail hardware store*] we recently listed for sale. It is located at [*105 Midvale*], and the price of [$ _____] includes [*all fixtures and an advantageous lease*]. The books are open to a qualified buyer [*, and owner financing is possible*].

I will call you in the next few days to ask for your help in identifying any of your customers who might be interested in an exceptional expansion opportunity.

Yours truly,

_____

Enclosure: [*Card*]

NOTE: *Suppliers have a stake in finding a buyer, because a happy buyer will feel indebted to the supplier.*

Many businesses are sold to buyers based on information gained from suppliers.

For a supplier letter, the business should be identified, and a price or price range should be indicated.

Chapter

9

Buyer Letters

Transmittal Letter—Requested Data

[*Date*]

_____
_____
_____

Dear _____ :

I have enclosed the information you requested [*concerning*]
[_____].

I will be calling you in the next few days to [*answer any questions
you may have / arrange to show you (this / these) fine property
(properties)*].

Yours truly,

_____

Enclosures: [*Card, Property information*]

Buyer Monthly Costs Estimate Worksheet

[*Date*]

_____

_____

_____

Dear _____ :

I have prepared the following estimate of the true monthly costs of home ownership, considering the tax benefits offered by home ownership.

The estimate is based on the following assumptions:

Purchase price	$ _____
Total closing costs	$ _____
Down payment	$ _____
Amount to be financed	$ _____

[_____]–year loan at [_____]% interest

Estimated Gross Monthly Costs

Principal and interest	$ (_____)
Property tax	$ (_____)
Homeowner insurance	$ (_____)
Other [*Association Dues*]	$ (_____)
Total estimated monthly gross costs	$ _____

Tax Benefits (Monthly)

Estimated deductible interest	$ _____
Estimated deductible property tax	$ _____
Monthly total tax deductions	$ _____
Estimated tax bracket (federal + state)	% _____
[_____]% × $ [_____] (monthly tax benefit) =	$ _____

Estimated Net Monthly Costs

Estimated gross
   monthly cost   _____

Estimated monthly
   tax benefits $(_____)

Monthly cost
   adjusted for tax benefits   _____

Although these costs are estimates only, I have tried to be as realistic as possible, and I believe that actual costs will not vary significantly from this estimate.

I will call you in a few days to discuss the estimate [*and to arrange some showings of homes that I believe will interest you*].

Yours truly,

_____

_____

NOTE: *You could prepare the Buyer Monthly Costs Estimate Worksheet as a form to use during a buyer qualifying session.*

Prospective Buyer—New Listing

[*Date*]

_____

_____

_____

Dear _____ :

[*I was unable to reach you by phone.*] We have just accepted a new listing, which I believe is exactly what you have been looking for. I want you to see this very special home before it is advertised to the general public.

Please call me at once. I wouldn't want you to miss this opportunity!

Yours truly,

_____

Enclosure: [*Card*]

NOTE: *Send this letter special delivery or overnight delivery. This letter creates a sense of urgency and sets a buying, rather than looking, mood. No information is given because, if it included anything buyers considered negative, they would not be eager to see the property.*

You can continue the tone of urgency by asking prospective buyers if they can take time off from work to see it. If they like the house, they will be happy they did.

Warning: Be reasonably certain that this is the house for your clients, or your credibility could be damaged.

Prospective Buyer—Price Reduction

[*Date*]

_____

_____

_____

Dear _____ :

The house you liked so much in [*Elmside*], the one with [*the huge fireplace and the fruit trees in the backyard*], has just been reduced in price. The original price set by the owners was [*$169,500*], but they have reduced this to [*$150,000*], a net reduction of [*$19,500*].

This reduction should result in a very quick sale. Because I would hate to see anyone else get this exceptional buy, I think you should take another look at this property. I will call you to arrange a showing of this home and another new listing that I think will interest you.

Yours truly,

_____

Enclosure: [*Card*]

NOTE: *While an initial phone call is superior to a letter, this letter would be appropriate for a prospective buyer living outside the area.*

Send this letter if the prospects indicated mild interest.

The mention of the other home is a final hook to set up the showings.

Offer to Out-of-Area Buyer

[*Date*]

_____

_____

_____

Dear _____ :

In accord with our [*telephone discussion on Wednesday, October 8th*], I have prepared a purchase offer for the property at [*111 Midvale Lane*]. The purchase offer reflects your offering price of [*$165,000*] and it [*includes terms / items that vary from the listing, and any special conditions*].

Please sign and return [*two*] copies of the purchase agreement to me as soon as possible along with [*your deposit check for $16,500*], which will be [*held uncashed until the offer is accepted*]. If the offer is not accepted, your deposit will be returned to you in full.

If the owners accept your offer, I believe that you will have made an exceptionally fine purchase. Even at the list price, I think that this [*home*] is an excellent buy.

Yours truly,

_____

Enclosures: [*Offer to purchase, Card*]

NOTE: *The last sentence really points the buyer toward looking favorably at a counteroffer.*

Acceptance to Buyer

[*Date*]

_____

_____

_____

Dear _____ :

Congratulations! Enclosed is a signed acceptance of your offer to purchase the property at [*55 Chestnut Street*].

I will be calling you in a few days to go over requirements for closing and to provide advice and assistance as needed.

You have purchased a [*home*] that I believe will provide you with much happiness.

Yours truly,

_____

Enclosure: [*Acceptance of offer to purchase*]

Rejection of Offer—No Counteroffer

[*Date*]

_____

_____

_____

Dear _____ :

[*Mr. and Mrs. Jones*] have indicated that they are unable to accept your offer to purchase their [*home*].

Although they would very much like to sell to you, they feel that the price they had set is more than reasonable based on the current real estate marketplace.

Because I feel very strongly that this [*home*] meets your needs better than any other [*home*] available and that the price asked is favorable, I have enclosed a new offer form reflecting that price.

If you wish to be the owner of this fine [*home*], please sign and return [*two*] copies of the offer in the envelope provided. [*It would be unfortunate to lose this fine opportunity for a difference of only about 5 percent.*]

I will call you in the next few days to answer any questions that you might have.

Yours truly,

_____

P.S. Keep in mind that long after the price has been forgotten you will be enjoying the [*amenities / advantages*] of this fine [*home*].

Enclosures: [*Offer to purchase*]

NOTE: *If at all possible, prospective buyers should be immediately notified by phone or in person of a rejection of their offer. If a phone call was made, start the letter with, "In accord with our telephone discussion . . . ."*

Counteroffer

[*Date*]

_____

_____

_____

Dear _____ :

[*As I said in our telephone conversation*], the owners, [*Mr. and Mrs. Smith*], were unable to accept your offer of [*$90,000*] for their property at [*55 Crescent Cove*]. [*They feel that they would be receiving far less than they would need to obtain replacement housing. | They feel they cannot take a loss of that magnitude. | Although they like you and would like you to be the new owners, they are just unable to accept your offer.*]

However, they have made an extremely attractive counteroffer, which would allow you to obtain an exceptional purchase. You will see that they have lowered their price by [*$20,000*]. If you sign and return [*two*] copies to our office by [give date], you will be the owner of a home you can truly be proud of at a price that is far less than I thought possible.

I will be calling you within a few days to answer any questions that you may have.

Yours truly,

_____

Enclosures: [*Counteroffer*]

NOTE: *If you are preparing a counteroffer to be presented by mail, we suggest that you use a new form so that the buyers need only sign, rather than initial and date, changes. The sellers should sign, and the places for buyer signatures should be checked with red ink.*

If you send the counteroffer by an express delivery service, it will increase the feeling that this counteroffer has value.

Buyer Purchase Cost Estimate

[Date]

_____

_____

_____

Dear _____ :

Enclosed is our Buyer Cost Estimate Worksheet.

While we believe that the estimates are reasonably reliable, they are not guaranteed.

If you have any questions, please call me.

Yours truly,

_____

Enclosure: *[Buyer Cost Estimate Worksheet]*

NOTE: *The Buyer Cost Estimate Worksheet is on page 196.*

Buyer Cost Estimate Worksheet

[*Clyde Realty*]
[*1627 W. Maple*]
[*Midtown, OR 91582*]
[*(318) 807-2136*]

Buyer Cost Estimate
Prepared for [*John and Sara Smith*]

Property: _____

Costs		Credits	
Purchase price	$ _____	Down payment $ _____	
Loan costs		Loans being	
Appraisal fee	$ _____	assumed (_____)	
Origination costs	$ _____	Seller financing (_____)	
Miscellaneous		Taxes	
fees	$ _____	(prorated) (_____)	
Impound account	$ _____	**Total credits** $ _____	
Insurance	$ _____		
Taxes (prorated)	$ _____		
Title insurance /			
abstracts	$ _____		
Attorney fees /			
escrow	$ _____		
Miscellaneous			
costs	$ _____		
Total costs	$ _____		
Total credits	$(_____)		
	$ _____ To be financed or paid		
	at closing		

Contingent Offer

[*Date*]

_____

_____

_____

Dear _____ :

Your offer-to-purchase agreement dated [_____] was contingent on [_____].

The purchase contract provides that if a subsequent written offer is accepted that is contingent on your rights, you shall have [*seven days*] to waive the contingencies set forth in your offer. You are hereby notified that a subsequent offer has been received and accepted. Unless the seller shall have received notice by [give date] that you have waived your contingencies, your offer shall terminate and become void, and your earnest money deposit shall be returned to you. You are also advised that such notification must be prompt.

A contingency release form is included for your signature if you wish to waive the contingencies in your purchase offer.

If you have any questions, please contact me immediately.

Yours truly,

_____

Enclosure: [*Contingency release form*]

cc: [*Owner*]

NOTE: *We suggest that this notice be sent either via registered mail with a return receipt requested or by express carrier, unless the offer prescribes another manner for delivery of notices.*

Problem with a Contract Condition— Buyer or Seller

[*Date*]

_____

_____

_____

Dear _____ :

[*As we agreed in our telephone discussion on* (give date*)]*, your purchase contract for the [*purchase / sale*] of [describe property and give address] requires that [state condition] be [*obtained / completed*] by [*August 1*].

[*You indicated / It is my understanding*] that the above condition has not yet been fulfilled. You therefore are at risk of the [*buyer / seller*] declaring you to be in default of your agreement [*which could result in damages*].

If there is any problem fulfilling the required condition, [*or if I can be of any help to you*], please contact me immediately so I can work with you toward a satisfactory solution.

Yours truly,

_____

Enclosure: [*Card*]

cc: [_____]

NOTE: *After a phone call, a letter should be used to document the problem. If there appears to be a problem, the other party should, of course, be notified.*

Buyer Failed Contingency

[*Date*]

_____

_____

_____

Dear _____ :

Your offer dated [*June 1, 1990*] to purchase the property at [*2736 Wright Road in Newton Heights*] was contingent on [*your obtaining a $100,000 loan with $10,000 down by July 15*]. You have been unable to [*obtain the required financing and have indicated that you are unable to waive the contingency*]. Therefore, in accord with your purchase offer, your offer has become null and void. With the concurrence of the owners, I am enclosing [*Clyde Realty*] trust account check No. [*2933*] in the amount of [*$5,000*], representing the full return of your earnest money deposit made with your offer to purchase.

If you have any questions or if I can serve you in any way, please contact me.

Yours truly,

_____

Enclosure: [*Check*]

cc: [Give owner's name.]

NOTE: *Obtain owner's concurrence in writing before earnest money is returned because of a failed contingency.*

Buyer Breach of Purchase Agreement

[*Date*]

_____

_____

_____

Dear _____ :

According to your purchase agreement with [*Mrs. James Smith*] dated [*June 1, 1990*], for the purchase of [*555 Midvale Court*], you were required to [*increase your deposit by $10,000*] no later than [*August 3, 1990*].

You have failed to meet your contractual obligation. Therefore, I have been authorized as the agent for [*Mrs. James Smith*] to inform you that your failure is a material breach of your agreement. The seller hereby declares the above contract to be null and void based on said breach.

[*Under said agreement, your deposit is to be forfeited as liquidated damages. Please sign and return the enclosed forms authorizing the release of your deposit to the sellers as liquidated damages. / The sellers reserve the right to bring legal action against you for damages suffered resulting from your breach of contract.*]

Yours truly,

_____

Enclosure: [*Release of deposit*]

[*cc: Mrs. James Smith*]

NOTE: *Do not send this letter without specific* written *authorization from the owners.* Always *check with your legal representative. Rights vary among states.*

Information to New Owner

[*Date*]

_____

_____

_____

Dear _____ :

To aid you in getting established in your new home, we have
included a list of phone numbers for utility hook-ups, [*cable TV*],
[*trash pickup*], and [*newspapers*], as well as some general area
information that we believe will be useful to you. If [*Clyde Realty*]
can be of any further assistance, don't hesitate to call me.

Yours truly,

_____

Enclosure: [*Lists, General information*]

NOTE: *In addition to phone numbers, consider area maps, school
information, information on all area houses of worship,
bus information, and so on. Your local chamber of commerce office can probably supply you with a large packet of
information for the new resident.*

Information on Utilities and Services

[*Date*]

_____

_____

_____

Dear _____ :

For your information, here are a few numbers that will help when you move into your new home:

Telephone service	_____
Gas connection	_____
Electrical service	_____
Water	_____
Cable TV	_____
Newspaper	_____
Trash service	_____
School registration	_____
[*Central District*]	_____
Emergency Numbers	
Fire	_____
Police	_____
Ambulance	_____
[Other]	_____

If you like, I would be happy to give you my recommendations for everything from an auto mechanic to a [*hairstylist*].

Sincerely,

_____

Enclosure: [*Card*]

School Registration Information

[*Date*]

_____

_____

_____

Dear _____ :

Just a quick note to let you know that you [*can now register Judy and Bobby*] for [*Midvale School starting July 10th*].

By registering early, you will avoid having to rush after you move in to your new home. I am certain that you will have plenty of other things to keep you busy.

Best regards,

_____

Enclosure: [*Card*]

Insurance Solicitation

[*Date*]

_____

_____

_____

Dear _____ :

The lender [*Midvale Savings and Loan*] will be requiring you to carry a fire policy on your new home in the amount of at least [*$100,000*]. We recommend that you consider a homeowner's policy in the amount of [$ _____], which would provide [$ _____] in liability coverage as well as insure your possessions up to [$ _____].

We also recommend replacement coverage that pays the full value of personal property, not just a depreciated value. Such coverage is available through your full-service insurance agent or, if you like, we can write the policy through our office and supply a copy to the lender. A policy providing the coverage we have recommended would cost [*$430 for one year*] if written through our office, with [*United Casualty*]. I have enclosed a brochure describing the policy.

I will be contacting you in the next few days to find out if you want our office to handle the insurance for you.

Yours truly,

_____

Enclosure: [*Insurance brochure*]

Buyer—Final Inspection

[*Date*]

_____

_____

_____

RE: [*Address*]

Dear _____ :

In accord with your purchase agreement, I have arranged for you to conduct a final [*walk-through inspection / inspection*] of the property on [*Tuesday, September 23, at 10 AM*].

[*I will meet you at the property. / You can of course bring a professional inspector with you.*] If for any reason you are not going to be available at this time, please contact me as soon as possible.

Yours truly,

_____

Enclosure: [*Card*]

Buyer/Seller Notice of Settlement Conference

[Date]

_____

_____

_____

Dear _____ :

The settlement conference for your [*sale / purchase*] of [*111 Midvale Lane*] has been scheduled for [*June 1, 1990*] at [*55 Sycamore Place, Suite 3301*].

[All (*buyers / sellers*) must attend so they can sign the (*mortgage / deed*).]

[*Please bring a cashier's check in the amount of $39,528. / See enclosed statement.*]

I am glad that we have been able to fulfill your needs [*and I look forward to seeing you at the closing*].

Yours truly,

_____

Enclosure(s): [*Settlement statement, Card*]

Buyer Notice of Settlement Conference

[*Date*]

_____

_____

_____

Dear _____ :

I have enclosed a statement showing total closing costs [*loans*] and the balance due at closing for your new home at [*111 Crescent Cove*].

[*Please bring a cashier's check in the amount of ($39,528) to the closing, made out to (James Smith)*]. The closing is scheduled for [*10 AM*] on [*Wednesday, April 3rd*], at [*3301 Sycamore Boulevard*]. I am glad that I was able to help you find such a fine home.

Yours truly,

_____

Enclosure: [*Closing statement*]

Closing Statement Transmittal

[*Date*]

_____

_____

_____

Dear _____ :

Enclosed is a copy of the closing statement for your [*sale of / purchase of*] [*6160 Jupiter Lane*].

[*I am certain that you will enjoy many happy years in your new home.*] If you or your friends have any future real estate needs, I hope that you will think of me.

Sincerely,

_____

Enclosure: [*Closing statement*]

Service Evaluation—Buyer after Sale

[Date]

_____

_____

_____

Dear _____:

To help us improve our service to buyers, we would appreciate if you would rate our services in the purchase of your home at [give address].

Buyer Evaluation of [*Clyde Realty*]

1. Do you feel that the real estate agent listened to you and really understood your needs?
   ☐ Yes   ☐ No

2. Do you feel that the agent was realistic in explaining the financial qualifications and down payment requirements for the home you purchased?
   ☐ Yes   ☐ No

3. Do you feel that the agent made efforts to find a home for you that best met your needs?
   ☐ Yes   ☐ No

4. Was the agent knowledgeable about homes shown, neighborhoods, market conditions and financing?
   ☐ Yes   ☐ No

5. Were calls to the agent or questions you raised promptly returned or answered to your satisfaction?
   ☐ Yes   ☐ No

6. Do you feel that the agent was honest in all of his or her dealings with you and helpful in preparing your purchase offer?
   ☐ Yes   ☐ No

7. After the acceptance of the offer, was the agent helpful in suggesting a lender or financing alternatives?
   ☐ Yes   ☐ No

8. Do you feel that the agent kept you adequately informed during the period from your offer until closing?
  ☐ Yes   ☐ No

9. Would you recommend the services of the agent to a friend who wanted to buy a home?
  ☐ Yes   ☐ No

10. Can we show this evaluation to other prospective buyers?
  ☐ Yes   ☐ No

11. Any additional comments: _____
  _____

Please return this evaluation in the enclosed, stamped envelope. Thank you very much for your assistance.

Yours truly,

_____

[*Clyde Realty*]

_____

NOTE: *Buyers usually develop a rapport with the selling agent. Since this is an evaluation of that agent, you will receive many "Yes" responses.*

With the buyers' approvals, an agent can show these evaluations to prospective buyers during the qualification process. Positive evaluations help sell the agent as someone who is very helpful to buyers.

Notice To Apply for Homeowner Tax Exemption

[*Date*]

_____

_____

_____

Dear _____ :

[*California*] offers a special property tax exemption for owner-occupied homes. You must, however, apply for this exemption by [*September 1*] for the 19[*94*] tax year. I have enclosed [*information on applying for the exemption / an exemption application*] for your convenience.

I would feel terrible if you did not receive the benefits you are entitled to. If you have any questions, please contact me.

Sincerely,

_____

Enclosure(s): [*Tax exemption application*]

NOTE: *In many states, a resident homeowner is entitled to special tax treatment, but the homeowner must apply for it.*

Insurance Solicitation—Mortgage Insurance

[*Date*]

_____

_____

_____

Dear _____ :

I hope that you are enjoying your lovely new home. You might be interested in the enclosed brochure. It concerns a mortgage insurance policy that will pay off your mortgage if you die or will make the payments for you if you become disabled. Because of your concern for your family, please consider this plan.

The premiums on your current mortgage at your age of [*39*] come to only [*$24*] a [*month*], and the payments are guaranteed to remain the same for the life of the loan.

I will be calling you in a few days to answer any questions you might have concerning this low-cost family protection.

Sincerely,

_____

Enclosure: [*Insurance brochure*]

NOTE: *If you sell mortgage insurance, a good time to sell is after the home sale has been closed. Before the sale, buyers are concerned about all the expenses of closing, and they are more reluctant to take on new debt.*

Mortgage insurance is actually decreasing term life insurance.

Buyer Purchased Through Another Broker

[*Date*]

_____

_____

_____

Dear _____ :

Congratulations! I was very happy to learn that you had found the [*home*] that fulfills your needs. Although I am sorry I was unable to locate that [*special home*] for you, I do wish you happiness in your new [*home*]. From what I know of the area, I am certain that you made a wise choice.

If you need real estate assistance in the future, don't hesitate to contact me. I am ready to use my best efforts on your behalf.

Sincerely,

_____

Enclosure: [*Card*]

NOTE: *This letter reestablishes the relationship for future referral calls or dealings. Otherwise, the buyers might avoid the agent because they believe he or she is angry with them for going elsewhere.*

Anniversary of Purchase

[*Date*]

_____

_____

_____

Dear _____ :

Although it is hard to realize, we are celebrating your anniversary this week! On [*June 1*], it will be exactly [*four*] years since [*I sold you your home / you purchased your home through our office*]. I hope that your home has been good to you in those years; [*I know that it has certainly appreciated in value*].

I will call you in a few days to ask for your help in identifying any of your friends who might need real estate services.

Happy anniversary!

_____

Enclosure: [*Card*]

Chapter

10

Property Management

Rental Inquiry

[*Date*]

_____
_____
_____

Dear _____ :

In response to your inquiry, we have the following units available
for [*June 1st occupancy / immediate occupancy*] that appear to meet
your stated requirements:

- [*Two-bedroom, two-bath at 1822 West Stevens, $430/month
  with $400 security deposit on a one-year lease (no pets).*]
- [*Two-bedroom at 731 West Third Street, $400/month with a
  $400 security deposit on a one-year lease.*]

I will be calling you in the next few days to discuss your real estate
needs and to arrange to show you available rental property in
[*Orchard Ridge*]. [*We also have several homes and condominiums
that can be purchased with very low and even no down payment and
with monthly payments within your indicated payment range*].

Yours truly,

_____

Enclosure: [*Card*]

Approval of Rental Application

[Date]

_____

_____

_____

Dear _____ :

Your rental application has been approved for [*733 West Third Street*] with occupancy on [*October 31st*].

Please come to [*our office*] by [*October 20*] to sign the lease and to pay the balance of the required deposits as follows:

[*Rent October 1–31*]	[*$480*]
[*Last month's rent*]	[*$480*]
[*Security deposit*]	[*$480*]
Total advance rent and deposits	[*$1,440*]
Less application deposit	[*($200)*]
Balance due:	[*$1,240*]

I look forward to seeing you.

Yours truly,

_____

Enclosure: [*Card*]

Rental Application Rejection #1

[Date]

_____

_____

_____

Dear _____ :

Enclosed is [*your check / our check*] in the amount of [*$200*], which constitutes the return of your rental application deposit for [give address][*less the nonrefundable credit report fee of* ($ _____).]

We have accepted another applicant for the premises.

[*We do have several other units available in other buildings:*]

Address	Size	Rental
[*1732 Third Street*	*2 BR 2 Bath*	*$600*]
[*501 Chestnut Circle*	*2 BR 1½ Bath*	*550*]
[*2001 Jupiter Avenue*	*2 BR 1 Bath*	*650*]

[*If you wish to view any of these units, please contact our office.*]

[*I will call you in the next few days to arrange to show you any of our offerings that interest you.*]

[*We also have a number of properties for sale with reasonable, low down payments. If you would like more information on these, please contact me.*]

Thank you for considering [*Clyde Realty*], and we hope you will be able to locate suitable housing.

Yours truly,

_____

NOTE: *By mentioning other housing opportunities, you lessen the likelihood that rental applicants will feel discriminated against. Of course, if the reason for rejection of the tenant was poor credit or rental history, you would not want to mention other properties. (See the following letter.)*

Rental Application Rejection #2

[*Date*]

_____

_____

_____

Dear _____ :

We regret to inform you that your rental application for [*2001 Jupiter Avenue*] has been rejected.

Enclosed is [*your check / our check*] for [*$300*], which represents the return of your rental deposit [*less the nonrefundable credit report fee of ($20) as agreed to in your rental application*].

If you have any questions, please contact me.

Yours truly,

_____

Enclosure: [*Check*]

cc: [*Resident property manager*]

NOTE: *We strongly suggest that you avoid listing reasons for rejecting applications in your letter, as they tend to lead to protracted confrontations. You should fully document your files, however, since applicants sometimes claim wrongful bias.*

Late Payment—Waiver of Late Charge

[*Date*]

_____

_____

_____

Dear _____ :

Your rent payment for the month of [$ _____] was due at our office on [give date]. However, we did not receive it until [give date].

A late charge of [$ _____] is authorized by paragraph [*six*] of your lease.

Since this is your first late payment, we will waive the late charge in this instance. However, it is essential that future rent payments be received on time. If any future rent payment is received late, a late charge will be assessed against you as provided by your lease agreement.

Yours truly,

_____

_____

Late Payment Charge

[*Date*]

_____

_____

_____

Dear _____ :

Your rent payment for the month of [give month] was due at our office on [give date]. It was not received until [give date].

You are hereby notified that in accord with paragraph [*four*] of your lease, you have been assessed a late charge of [$ _____].

Please remit this amount immediately. Thank you.

Yours truly,

_____

_____

Bad Check

[*Date*]

_____

_____

_____

Dear _____ :

Your check no. [_____] in the amount of [$ _____]
made out to [_____] has been returned to us from
your bank marked insufficient funds.

Please see that this office is furnished with either cash, a money
order, cashier's check or certified check in the amount of
[$ _____] by [_____]. [*This amount includes a
charge of ($25.00) for the returned check, under the terms of your
lease, as well as a late charge of ($25.00)*]. Failure to comply shall
be regarded as a breach of your legal obligations.

Yours truly,

_____

NOTE: *No threat of legal action is made, although it might possibly be inferred. A date is set to express urgency. The letter
makes clear that a personal check will not be accepted.*

Rent Increase #1

[*Date*]

_____

_____

_____

Dear _____ :

Because of [*increased expenses / increased interest rates / improvements we have made*], a rental adjustment has become necessary.

As of [*May 1*], the rent for [*5800 Crescent Cove, #3-S*] will be increased from the current [*$600*] per month to [*$625*] per month.

Yours truly,

_____

cc: [*Resident property manager*]

NOTE: *Be certain that notices comply with your state laws as to content, notice period and service of the notice (registered mail might be required).*

Rent Increase #2

[Date]

_____

_____

_____

Dear _____ :

You are hereby notified [*in accord with Arizona law*] that as of [*January 1, 1990*], your rent shall be increased from [*$600*] per month to [*$625*] per month for the premises at [*643 Jupiter Lane, second floor*].

Yours truly,

_____

cc: [*Resident property manager*]

NOTE: *Make certain that rent increase notices are given for the statutory period. For example, a number of states require that notification be given at least 30 days before the rent increase, and in some states the notification period must end on the day rent is due.*

Consider using registered or certified mail, and request return receipts. This avoids the claim of nondelivery or of your notice being mistaken for an advertisement. Your state statutes may specify the manner of delivering the notice as well as the form of the notice.

Complaint about Tenant's Breach of Rules

[*Date*]

_____

_____

_____

Dear _____ :

We have received a complaint that

[_____

_____]

[, *which has been confirmed by our resident manager*]. Of course, this violates [*the occupancy rules you signed at the time you leased the premises / your lease*].

Apartment dwellers must live in proximity to others. It is therefore necessary that each resident respect the rights of others. If there are further problems, it could result in the necessity of eviction procedures under the provisions of your lease agreement.

Yours truly,

_____

cc: [*Resident property manager*]

_____

Notice To Cease Prohibited Activity

[*Date*]

_____

_____

_____

Dear _____ :

It has come to our attention that [*you have been performing major automobile repair work in your parking space at 110 Stardust Lane*].

This is a violation of [*your lease / the occupancy rules and regulations you signed at the time of rental*].

You are hereby ordered to cease this activity immediately, or corrective action shall be required in accord with your lease.

Yours truly,

_____

cc: [*Resident property manager*]

Letter to Resident Manager—Problem

[*Date*]

_____

_____

_____

Dear _____:

[*An inspection of the property at (* _____ *) revealed the following deficiency(deficiencies):*]

[*We have received a complaint regarding the following:*]

- _____
- _____
- _____
- _____

Please rectify the [*problem(s) / deficiency(deficiencies)*] [*as soon as practical / immediately*].

If you have any questions, please contact me.

Yours truly,

_____

Notice to Tenant—
Failure To Maintain Exterior or Lawn

[*Date*]

_____

_____

_____

Dear _____ :

In [*driving by* / *inspecting*] the [*home at 12 West Davis Street*], which you are renting from our office, I was surprised to see that [*the lawn has not been cared for*].

Under the terms of your lease, you are required to [*maintain the landscaping*]. Unless [*the lawn is properly maintained by August 1st*], we shall have to contract for the work with [*a gardening service*] and add the charges to your rent.

Yours truly,

_____

Notice of Lease Automatic Renewal

[*Date*]

_____

_____

_____

Dear _____ :

Your present lease for [*the two-bedroom house*] at [*660 Stardust Circle*] expires on [*April 1, 1995*].

This is to remind you that unless you give notice to the contrary by [*March 1, 1995*], the lease by its terms will be automatically extended for [*another year*]. If you have any questions, please contact me.

Yours truly,

_____

cc: [*Resident property manager*]

NOTE: *Although many owners don't remind tenants of the automatic renewal, the reminder does avoid hard feelings and future problems.*

Lease Expiration Notice—New Lease

[*Date*]

_____

_____

_____

Dear _____ :

Your lease for [*660 Maple Lane*] expires on [*April 1, 1995*]. I have enclosed a new lease for the premises substantially the same as your old lease [*at the same rent / except that the rent has been increased to $625. The higher rent is required because of cost increases in the operation and management of the property*].

Please sign and return [*two*] copies of the new lease to my office by [*March 1, 1995*]. If I do not receive your new lease by this date, I will assume that you do not wish to remain in possession and appropriate notices will then be given.

Yours truly,

_____

Enclosure: [*Lease*]

cc: [*Resident apartment manager*]

NOTE: *Although it is not necessary to give reasons for a rent increase, a reason makes your action seem less arbitrary and helps to maintain better tenant relations.*

Tenant Notice of Leaving in Violation of Lease

[Date]

_____

_____

_____

Dear _____ :

Your current lease, dated *[January 1, 1994]* does not expire until *[January 1, 1995]*. If you wish to vacate the premises before this date, you will be held liable for the cost of re-renting the premises as well as any rental loss incurred.

If you wish to locate a tenant to assume your lease obligations, we will allow a lease assignment subject to our approval based on our reasonable rental criteria. You, of course, would remain liable if the new tenant defaults on the lease.

Please contact me immediately about your intentions. If you are vacating on *[September 1, as you indicated]*, I want to begin immediately to find a new tenant in order to keep your legal obligations to a minimum.

Yours truly,

_____

cc: *[Resident apartment manager]*

Tenant Vacated in Violation of Lease

[*Date*]

_____

_____

_____

Dear _____ :

I have been informed that on [*April 15*] you vacated the premises at [*1700 Sycamore Avenue*]. [*Your lease required a 30-day notice, which was not given. / Your lease does not expire until (June 1).*] Therefore, you shall be held liable [*for the rental until the end of the lease period / for the 30-day notice period expiring May 15*].

If we are able to re-rent the premises prior to the above date, your liability will be reduced by the rent received for said period less the costs of re-renting the premises.

Please contact this office immediately to make arrangements for fulfilling your obligation.

Yours truly,

_____

cc: [*Resident apartment manager*]

NOTE: *This letter might require modification based on state law. Contact legal counsel.*

Notice To Vacate

[*Date*]

_____

_____

_____

Dear _____ :

In accord with [*the terms of your tenancy / Arizona law*], you are hereby notified that you are ordered to vacate the premises at [*6603 Sycamore Parkway*] by [*May 1, 1990*]. This notice shall constitute the [*30-day notice*] required by [*state law*].

Agent for: [*Clyde Management*]

_____

cc: [*Resident manager*]

NOTE: *Be certain that your notice and the service of the notice conforms with your state law. Registered mail or personal service might be required. You may have to post the notice on the door to the premises. In some states, the notification period must end on the day rent is due. Check with an attorney, and then modify the notice if required.*

Acknowledgment of Tenant's Notice To Vacate

[*Date*]

_____

_____

_____

Dear _____ :

We acknowledge your notice to vacate the premises at [*3120 West Lincoln, Unit 8*] by [*March 1, 1995*].

You will be called by [*the manager, Mr. Jones / this office*] to arrange to show your [*apartment*] to prospective renters. We will try to give you as much notice as possible.

Yours truly,

_____

cc: [*Resident property manager*]

Tenant Letter—End-of-Lease Inspection

[*Date*]

_____

_____

_____

Dear _____ :

In accord with [*your notice / our notice / the rental agreement*], you will be vacating the premises at [_____] on [*April 30*].

We will be conducting an inspection of the premises at [*2:00 PM*], [*April 30*] to determine whether there is any damage to the premises other than normal wear and tear [*and whether any items are missing from the premises*]. [*After this inspection / Within _____ days of this inspection*], your security deposit will be returned to you minus deductions for any damage to the premises [*or for any missing items*].

If you wish, you may be present for this inspection.

Yours truly,

_____

cc: [*Resident manager*]

NOTE: *This letter reminds tenants that they should leave the premises in good condition, and it will probably reduce the cleaning requirements prior to re-renting.*

Notice to Tenant of Damage
on Vacating Premises

[*Date*]

_____

_____

_____

Dear _____ :

Inspection of the premises at [*6603 Sycamore, third floor*] that you vacated on [*April 1*] revealed that [*the living room floor is scratched in several places, the ceiling fan and miniblinds from the dining room are missing, and the bathroom mirror is broken*].

Since the [*damages / missing articles*] are not normal wear and tear, we have made the necessary [*repairs / replacements*] and have deducted the cost from your [*property damage bond*]. [*The balance of ($75) is enclosed.*]

[*Since the cost of (repairs / replacements) exceeds the amount of your property damage bond, please remit ($300) to this office no later than (4 PM) on (April 10).*]

[*The necessary (repairs / replacements) have resulted in costs of ($300). Please remit this amount to our office no later than (4 PM) on (April 10).*]

Yours truly,

_____

Enclosure: [*Property damage bond statement*]

cc: [*Resident manager*]

NOTE: *By using a definite date for the alternative paragraphs, the former tenant will assume that legal action will be taken if the remittance is not paid by this date, although no threat is being made.*

Tenant Complaint—Forwarded for Action

[*Date*]

_____

_____

_____

Dear _____ :

I have received your [*letter*] about [*the unauthorized parking in your space*].

I have forwarded your concerns to [*the resident manager*]. [*He / She*] will be contacting you directly.

I sincerely hope that the problem is resolved to your satisfaction. If you have any other questions, call the manager or me.

Yours truly,

_____

cc: [*Resident manager*]

Tenant Complaint—Action Taken

[*Date*]

_____

_____

_____

Dear _____ :

I have received your [*letter*] about [*unauthorized parking in your space*].

[*The offending party has been contacted*], and we hope that the [*problem has been resolved*]. If the problem continues, please contact [*me directly / Mr. Brown, the building manager*].

Yours truly,

_____

cc: [*Mr. Brown*]

Tenant Complaint—No Action Taken

[*Date*]
_____
_____
_____

Dear _____ :

I have received your complaint [*that the neighbor's children have been disturbing you. Since we rent to families, the noise of children playing must be expected, although it can be exasperating at times.*]

[*Because we are unable to solve your problem, we would be willing to allow you to break your lease upon (30) days' notice. Please let me know what you decide.*]

[*When your lease expires, we would be happy to help you find a unit that better meets your requirements.*]

Yours truly,

_____

cc: [*Resident manager*]

Notice to Tenant of Lessor Entry

[*Date*]

_____

_____

_____

Dear _____ :

In accord with the terms of our lease, we will be [*making an inspection of the premises / showing the premises to a prospective buyer / repairing the kitchen floor in your unit*] at [*9 AM*] on [*Tuesday, February 6*].

If you are unable to be there at that time, please contact [*this office / Mr. Brown, the Building Manager*] so a more convenient time can be arranged [*so we can make certain that the building manager has all necessary keys*].

Yours truly,

_____

cc: [*Building manager*]

Notice of Work on Premises

[*Date*]

_____

_____

_____

Dear _____ :

In the next [*few days / few weeks*], we will be [*painting the lobby / replacing the air conditioning*]. We hope that you will not be inconvenienced by the work, which will be confined to normal working hours.

[*Access to your apartment will be required on (April 15). If you are not home, our resident manager, (Jane Smith), will remain in your unit while workers are present. (Please provide keys to the manager if required).*]

Yours truly,

_____

cc: [*Resident manager*]

NOTE: *This letter serves another purpose, in that it informs the tenants they are getting something for their rent; the owner is putting money back into the building. This service makes a subsequent rent increase more palatable to the tenants.*

Confirmation of Telephone Work Order

[*Date*]

_____

_____

_____

Dear _____ :

This will confirm our agreement on [*May 10*] for you to [*provide a pest control inspection*] at [*6501 Crescent Circle*]. It is understood that the work must be completed by [*June 1*].

[*Please call our office 24 hours before you begin work so we can be certain someone will be present to provide access to the property.*]

We acknowledge that your charge for said work shall be [*$125*].

[*Work order number (1073) has been assigned to this project. Please reference said work order in any billing or other correspondence.*]

[*Bill (this office / Mr. and Mrs. James) for the work no later than (July 1).*]

Yours truly,

_____

cc: [*Resident manager*]

Repair Request to Owner—
Authorization Required

[*Date*]

_____

_____

_____

Dear _____ :

Your property at [_____] requires the following repairs:

[_____

_____].
[*The cost for this work will be ($ _____) / The cost for this work is likely to exceed ($ _____) based on the enclosed (estimate / bid).*]

Our management contract requires your authorization for any repair that exceeds [$ _____]. We therefore request your authorization to make the required repairs. Failure to authorize repairs could result in [*vacancies and loss of income / damage to the property / being cited for code violations*].

Your prompt attention to this matter would be appreciated.

Yours truly,

_____

Enclosure: [*Bid*]

cc: [*Resident Manager*]

Chapter

11

Letters
to Other Brokers

Welcome to New Broker

[*Date*]

_____

_____

_____

Dear _____ :

As a fellow [*real estate broker / REALTOR®*] I would like to welcome you to [*the growing West Side*].

I am certain that we will have many productive dealings in the coming years, since cooperation is the basis of real estate success. I will stop by to meet you personally in a few weeks after you are settled.

I wish you success in your new office—welcome!

Sincerely,

_____

MLS Caravan—Breakfast or Lunch

[*Date*]

_____
_____
_____

Dear _____ :

CARAVAN—[*October 28th*]

Be sure to visit [*37 West Toliver Avenue*] (see property brief attached), and be my guest for a

**[*Continental Breakfast /
Breakfast Buffet /
Very Special Brunch /
Luncheon Buffet*]**

from [*9 AM–11 AM*]

Sincerely,

_____

Enclosure: [*Property brief*]

NOTE: *In areas where there are more listings than agents can possibly visit, you may need something extra to bring in agents. Food will act as a magnet in these situations.*

Invitation—Agent Open House

[*Date*]

_____

_____

_____

Dear _____ :

YOU ARE INVITED

To a very special agent-only

OPEN HOUSE

at

[_____]

[*Property Brief Attached*]

From [*4–7 PM*]

[*Friday, April 3rd*]

[*Buffet Dinner / Refreshments*]

[*Drawing for Valuable Door Prizes /
3 Electronic Tape Measures
To Be Given Away*]

RSVP   [*John Jones 346-8041*]

NOTE: *An RSVP will usually increase attendance because it makes
the invitation more special to the recipients, and once they*

Office Open House Invitation

[*Clyde Realty*]

Open House

[*922 West Broadway*]

[*Wednesday, April 5*]

[*5–8 PM*]

Come visit with us at our [*new office /
new branch office*].

Refreshments will be served!

NOTE: *This invitation could be sent to owners, investors, escrow
and title companies, lenders, as well as other brokers and
salespeople.*

*We suggest that you have this invitation printed on regular
invitation stock.*

Referral Thank-You

[Date]

_____

_____

_____

Dear _____ :

Thank you very much for referring [*Jane Smith*] to this office.

I have shown [*the Smiths*] a number of properties [*and I am confident I will be able to meet their housing needs*].

[*I hope I will be sending you a check within a short time.*]

If I can ever be of service to you, don't hesitate to call me.

Yours truly,

_____

_____

Referral Thank-You—No Sale

[*Date*]

_____

_____

_____

Dear _____ :

Thank you very much for referring [*Joseph Jones*] to our office. Although we contacted [*the Jones's*] promptly [*and showed them a number of homes*], they purchased a home from [*another agent / a builder*].

I want you to know that our failure was not the result of lack of effort. In fact, if there is another opportunity, I would like to show you that [*Clyde Realty*] does make sales and is worthy of your referrals.

Yours truly,

_____

_____

Referral—Notice of Sale

[*Date*]

_____

_____

_____

Dear _____ :

Just a note to let you know that [*Sylvia Smith*], whom you referred to us, has [*purchased a home through this office*]. The closing is scheduled for [*June 1*]. On closing, we will immediately forward your referral fee of [$ _____] based on our office commission of [$ _____].

We appreciate the referral and look forward to future cooperation with your office.

Yours truly,

_____

Referral Fee—Transmittal

[*Date*]

_____

_____

_____

Dear _____ :

Enclosed is our check in the amount of [$ _____] for your referral of [*John Jones*] as well as our commission statement.

We look forward to working with you in the future.

Yours truly,

_____

Enclosures: [*Check, Commission statement*]

Seeking an Investment Property

[*Date*]

_____

_____

_____

Dear _____ :

I am working with a prospective investor who has [*more than $500,000*] to invest and desires [*residential property / commercial property / a raw-land investment*]. My buyer's primary objective is [*appreciation / income / tax-sheltered income*]. [*Safety is, of course, a consideration as well.*]

My investor [*wants a positive cash flow / will except a negative cash flow / wants at least a break-even cash flow*] with an [*all-cash / moderately leveraged / highly leveraged*] investment.

If you have any property listed with your office that you believe would interest my buyer, I would very much like to work with you.

Yours truly,

_____

Enclosure: [*Card*]

Request for Commission

[*Date*]

_____

_____

_____

Dear _____ :

[*On the morning of October 12, Mrs. Jean Jacobs of our office
showed a home that you have listed at 1112 Kings Drive to Mr. and
Mrs. William Apple. That afternoon, you held an Open House at the
same property, and Mr. and Mrs. William Apple stopped at the
house. They told your salesperson, Jim Peters, that they had seen the
house that morning with Mrs. Jacobs. Mr. Peters proceeded to prepare a purchase agreement, which the Apples signed and the owner
accepted.*] These facts, which can be fully verified, clearly indicate
that [*Clyde Realty*] is the procuring cause for the sale and is entitled
to the sales commission. We therefore expect your check in the
amount of [*$3,000*].

Yours truly,

_____

_____

NOTE: *An attempt to resolve a problem such as this should preferably be made in person or by phone before this letter is
sent.*

Broker Commission Split—Transmittal

[*Date*]

_____

_____

_____

Dear _____ :

Enclosed is our check for [$ _____], which represents [*50*] percent of the total commission for [*your sale*] of the property located at [*5 Sycamore Circle*] to [*Janet Smith*].

I have enclosed a copy of the closing statement for your records.

Your cooperation was greatly appreciated, and I look forward to writing many more checks such as this.

Yours truly,

_____

Enclosures: [*Check, Closing statement*]

Breach of Procedure by Our Office

[*Date*]

_____

_____

_____

Dear _____ :

I want to apologize personally to you for an unfortunate breach of procedure by our office. [*On June 16, one of our salespeople contacted one of your owners, Janet Smith, without going through your office / One of our salespeople contacted James Smith, whose listing was in full effect with your office, about obtaining a listing.*] The reasons for the breach and the fact that at the time the salesperson did not realize that [*he / she*] was in breach of ethics does not matter.

What does matter is that one of my salespeople failed to respect your rights. I want you to know that I will do everything in my power to make certain that such an action is not repeated.

Yours truly,

_____

_____

Breach of Procedure by Your Office

[*Date*]

_____

_____

_____

Dear _____ :

I am sorry to have to inform you that on [*August 21*] your salesperson, [*Sylvia Smith*], [*contacted James Smith, whose listing was in full effect with our office, about obtaining a listing*].

This type of action cannot be condoned because, in our profession, cooperation is the basis of success. We hope that such action is not repeated in the future.

Yours truly,

_____

_____

Arbitration Notice

[*Date*]

_____

_____

_____

Dear _____ :

Based on your failure to [*pay Clyde Realty the selling commission for the sale of 1112 Kings Drive to Mr. and Mrs. William Apple*], we are requesting arbitration of this matter with [*the San Marco Board of REALTORS® in accord with board rules and regulations*].

Yours truly,

_____

_____

NOTE: *Mandatory arbitration is possible when both parties are members of the organization that requires arbitration.*

Chapter

12

Letters Dealing with Conflict

Official Inquiry—Complaint

[*Date*]

_____

_____

_____

Dear _____ :

We have received your letter of [*June 3*]. I was very surprised that a complaint was made to your office. I have set forth the facts in the attachment and have included signed statements from those in our office who are involved.

Although we believe the complaint is entirely without merit, you can nevertheless expect our full cooperation in this matter. If you have any further questions, please do not hesitate to contact me.

Yours truly,

_____

Enclosures: [*Statement of fact, Agent statement(s)*]

General Complaint

[*Date*]

_____

_____

_____

Dear _____ :

I am very sorry that you have not been satisfied with the services of [*Clyde Realty*]. Although we don't always succeed, we nevertheless strive in good faith to meet the needs of both clients and customers. Our failures are actually important, because they stimulate us to improve.

I want you to know that my door is open to you at any time to discuss any problems freely, and I would be happy to meet with you at your convenience.

Yours truly,

_____

Buyer or Seller Complaint

[*Date*]

_____

_____

_____

Dear _____ :

Although I am sorry to hear of your dissatisfaction with the services of one of our salespeople, I am nevertheless glad that you brought this matter to my attention.

You can be assured that your complaint will be fully investigated and appropriate action will be taken consistent with the circumstances. Since we serve the public and our stock in trade is public trust, I will not tolerate even a hint of impropriety. If you have any questions, please call me.

Yours truly,

_____

Offer To Arbitrate

[*Date*]

_____

_____

_____

Dear _____ :

[*Clyde Realty*] would like to resolve [*your complaint*] in a fair and equitable manner. What could be more fair than to submit our disagreement to an impartial arbitrator for binding arbitration? If this appears satisfactory to you, please contact me, and we will work out the details of selecting an arbitrator.

[*As an alternative, in the interest of expediency we would agree to pay you ($3,000) for an immediate settlement.*]

Yours truly,

_____

_____

NOTE: *The optional second paragraph could save you time and money. However, settlement offers should be made in person, if practical.*

Offer of Settlement

[*Date*]

_____

_____

_____

Dear _____ :

Based on [*your letter of July 13 / our phone conversation on July 13*], it is clear that you feel [*Clyde Realty*] has not treated you in a fair and proper manner.

While I sincerely believe our actions were at all times fair and professional, I am nevertheless disturbed by your feelings toward us. We consider ourselves a part of the community, and we want very much to maintain a harmonious relationship with all of our neighbors.

[*Therefore, I am willing to (reduce our fee by $3,000 / pay one-half the cost of the damaged roof / remit to you one-half of the March rent).*]

[*I will contact you in the next few days to arrange a meeting to resolve this problem in a satisfactory manner.*]

[*Please let me know if my proposal meets with your approval.*]

Yours truly,

_____

Notification to State Department of Real Estate about Violation of the Law

[*Date*]

_____
_____
_____

Dear _____ :

I am sorry to report an apparent violation of our state real estate law by [*one of my associates / a licensed real estate agent*].

[*On April 12, 1989, Mr. Timothy Jones, a real estate salesperson licensed under my broker's license, accepted a $5,000 cash deposit from Mr. Kermit Pugh. Mr. Jones has not contacted our office since he received the deposit and has not been home in the four days since he accepted the deposit. We therefore assume that Mr. Jones has appropriated the deposit for his own use. We have notified the district attorney of these facts.*]

We will fully cooperate with your office in any investigation and will promptly supply any additional information requested.

Yours truly,

_____

Chapter

13

Personnel Letters

Real Estate Career Night Announcement

Join Us for Real Estate Career Night

- Learn how many people have found new direction in their lives through real estate.
- Learn the benefits that a professional career in real estate offers:

✓ The joy of helping others
✓ The independence of planning your own work
✓ Financial rewards directly related to your success in helping meet housing needs
✓ Constant mental stimulation

If you are a retiree, a homemaker reentering the work force, a recent graduate or simply interested in a career change, this is your opportunity to learn how a real estate career can meet your needs and to ask any questions you might have.

Thursday, April 8th

7:00 PM

Clyde Realty

473 N. Main

[*RSVP*]   [*555-8200*]

NOTE: *This notice can be mailed on invitation stock as an invitation or mailed as a letter. It can also be used as a flyer. Good places to leave or post flyers are employment offices, senior centers, and other public places.*

New or Prospective
Real Estate Salesperson Solicitation

[*Date*]

_____

_____

_____

Dear _____ :

I understand you [*are currently enrolled in a real estate license preparatory course / have applied to take your real estate salesperson's examination / have recently passed your real estate salesperson's examination*]. I wish you success, and I hope you find a career in real estate is as personally rewarding as it has been for many of us.

[*Clyde Realty*] is looking for people who are sincerely seeking a career and not just a job. People who want professional growth so they can meet the needs of others. People with integrity and motivation.

If you feel your goals are compatible with ours, I would like to meet with you to discuss various career options and to let you learn about us as we learn about you.

[*Please call me for a personal appointment. / I will be contacting you in the next few days to arrange a personal meeting so you can learn more about a career with (Clyde Realty).*]

Sincerely,

_____

_____

NOTE: *Some states sell lists of names of applicants for licensing examinations, as well as lists of names of those who passed their examinations. Some license preparatory schools will also provide names of students.*

Salesperson Solicitation—Retired

[*Date*]

_____

_____

_____

Dear _____ :

Are you

Tired of Being Retired?

If you like people, have good character, and are not afraid to start a new career, I would like to meet with you.

I can offer you the personal satisfaction of helping others, a feeling of self-worth working in an independent environment, mental stimulation and financial rewards earned by your success. After a short license-training program, we will work with you and guide you on your career.

[*Interested? Then call me today so we can meet to discuss your career in real estate.*]

[*Interested? I will call you in the next few days to discuss the benefits of a career in real estate.*]

Yours truly,

_____

NOTE: *This letter can be mailed to people living in retirement-oriented developments or modified for use as a flyer and distributed in retirement communities as well as in senior centers.*

Welcome New Agent
(Large or Multi-Office Broker)

[Date]

_____

_____

_____

Dear _____ :

Welcome to [*Clyde Realty*]!

Our goal at [*Clyde Realty*] is to serve the needs of buyers and sellers
to the best of our abilities. To accomplish this goal, we must be
knowledgeable professionals. Therefore, we encourage your professional growth, and we will do all we can to guide you in your success.

I look forward to a long and mutually beneficial association. If any
problems arise or if we can provide any assistance, please let us
know.

Sincerely,

_____

Training Session Notice

[*Clyde Realty*] Memo

Attention All Sales Personnel!

Training Session:

[*Wednesday, April 1, 9 AM–10 AM (Prior to Caravan)*]

Subject: [*Listing Techniques*]

[*If you are unable to attend, please contact Jane Jones
as soon as possible.*]

[*Coffee and rolls will be served.*]

NOTE: If the firm has multiple offices, include the location of the
session.

Sales Meeting Notice

[*Clyde Realty*] Memo

Attention: All Sales Personnel

Sales Meeting: [*Monday, June 17, 7 AM–8:30 AM*]

[*Coffee and donuts will be served.*]

If you cannot attend for any reason, please notify [*John Jones.*]

NOTE: *For regular sales meetings, a form can be used with the date inserted*

If the firm has multiple offices, include the location of the meeting.

Notice to Salesperson of Missed Meeting

[Date]

_____

_____

_____

Dear _____ :

You were missed at the [*training session on Wednesday, April 1, as well as the office meeting and property caravan on Wednesday, April 8.*] If you have any difficulties, I would be happy to provide any advice or assistance that I can offer.

Our office works as a team, and we try to help each other. We also view training and office meetings as important functions to aid all personnel.

I want every team member to share his or her knowledge, experience, and support with others. I look forward to your attendance and support in the future.

Sincerely,

_____

_____

NOTE: *Whenever possible, handle personnel matters in person rather than by letter.*

Notice to Salesperson—Unauthorized Absence

[*Date*]

_____

_____

_____

Dear _____ :

On [*Wednesday, March 1*], you were scheduled for [*floor time / an open house at 111 Circle Drive*]. You were not present, and I was not notified you would be absent so other arrangements could be made.

When a salesperson misses [*floor time, we have inadequate coverage of our calls. This results in wasted advertising dollars and lost opportunities. / an open house, not only do we waste advertising dollars, but we could have angry owners and angrier potential buyers who have made a trip to see a home that is not open*].

Although I realize there are legitimate emergencies, nevertheless it is imperative that the office be notified as soon as possible of any absence when you are scheduled to be present.

Sincerely,

_____

_____

NOTE: *A personal meeting is the preferred way to handle a matter such as this.*

Problem Notification

[*Date*]

_____

_____

_____

Dear _____ :

I am sorry to say that I have received a complaint about
[_____].

[*Could you please meet with me / Could you please meet with our
attorney and me*] on [*Friday, April 12 at 4 PM*] at [*5 Crescent
Boulevard, Suite 1800*]?

[*I have arranged a meeting between (Mr. Jones, you, and me) at
(our office) at (4 PM on Thursday, April 12).*] [*If you could come at
(3 PM), it will give me a chance to get all the facts straight.*]

Yours truly,

_____

Commission Dispute Between Agents

[*Date*]

_____

_____

_____

Dear _____ :

I would like to meet with you and [*Charles*] in my office on [*April 1*], at [*4 PM*], to resolve the disagreement over the entitlement to [*listing / sales*] commission for the [*listing of / sale of*] [*111 West Jackson Street*].

Sincerely,

_____

_____

Office Dispute Decision

[*Date*]

_____

_____

_____

Dear _____ :

According to your [*employment / independent contractor*] agreement with [*Clyde Realty*], commission disputes within the office will be resolved by [*binding broker arbitration*].

On [*April 11*], I heard your claim for [*one-half of the sales commission for the sale of the property at 111 West Jackson Street, as well as the claim of Emily Jones for the entire sales commission for the same sale*].

My decision in this case is that [*Emily Jones is entitled to the entire sales commission for the sale of 111 West Jackson Street*].

Sincerely,

_____

NOTE: *This letter can be used only if the salesperson's contract calls for binding arbitration by the broker.*

Salesperson Congratulations

[*Date*]

_____

_____

_____

Dear _____ :

Congratulations on [*your first sale over $1,000,000 / your first exchange / exceeding your sales goal for February / being the top (selling / listing) salesperson in our office for the month of (February)*]!

I hope this accomplishment is merely a prelude to even greater achievements. Use this as just one stepping stone to the future.

Warmest regards,

_____

Special Recognition—Training Completion or Professional Designation

[*Date*]

_____

_____

_____

Dear _____ :

You may be justifiably proud of your accomplishments in [*completing the Certified Residential Specialist (CRS) program / attaining the professional designation of Graduate of the REALTORS® Institute (GRI)*]. I know that it wasn't easy, but I am sure the feeling of confidence, prestige within the industry and, most importantly, the ability to better serve buyers and sellers makes the time well spent.

Congratulations—not just from me, but from our entire profession!

Sincerely,

_____

_____

Salesperson Award

[*Date*]

_____

_____

_____

Dear _____ :

This is to inform you that you are the grand winner of [*salesperson of the month for January*]. This award was achieved with [*your sales of $2,851,000*].

You can claim the award of [*a three-day, Las Vegas holiday for two*] at [*Anderson Travel*].

Our warmest congratulations,

_____

NOTE: *Awards should generally be made before the entire sales force. If a notice is used, the notice should be by telegram, express carrier service, or special delivery letter to emphasize the importance of the achievement.*

Happy Birthday #1

[*Date*]

_____

_____

_____

Dear _____ :

Well, another year has passed. In retrospect, it has been a good year for you. You are respected by your fellow workers as a knowledgeable and caring person. You are dedicated and have taken the reins of your own destiny. Most important, we regard you as our friend.

A very Happy Birthday, [*Martin*], from all of us!

_____   _____

_____   _____

_____   _____

NOTE: *A letter is a warmer approach than just a card. A small gift such as a quality pen or daily planner might be appropriate.*

Happy Birthday #2

Happy Birthday, [*Clarence*]!

We all wish you the very best
on your birthday:

Good Health

Good Friends

[*Happy Family*]

Prosperity

We hope you are with us at [*Clyde Realty*] to celebrate a
great many more of them. Again—a very Happy Birthday!

NOTE: *The entire staff should sign. The card could be attached to a metallic helium balloon anchored on the agent's desk with a box of candy or other small gift.*

Wedding Anniversary

[*Date*]

_____

_____

_____

Dear _____ :

My very best wishes to both of you on your wedding anniversary!
As a small token of my personal regard for you, I have enclosed
[*a certificate for dinner for two at the Golden Palm*].

It is my sincere hope that you have a joyful celebration of this and
many more anniversaries.

Very sincerely,

_____

_____

NOTE: *Include both the husband's and wife's names in the
salutation.*

Anniversary with Firm

[*Date*]

_____

_____

_____

Dear _____ :

I don't know if you noticed, but it's our anniversary. On [*June 1*], it will have been [*five*] years since you joined [*Clyde Realty*]. These years have been filled with many successes and a lot of hard work. During this time, you have helped to make possible the dream of home ownership for many families.

I want you to realize that your efforts have not gone unnoticed or unappreciated. I am proud to have you with the firm and look forward to a great many more anniversaries.

Congratulations!

_____

Birth of Son or Daughter

[*Date*]

_____

_____

_____

Dear _____ :

My warmest congratulations on the birth of your [*daughter / son*]!
Little [*Mary Elizabeth / John Martin*] has a [*father / mother*] [*she /
he*] can be proud of.

This small gift is a token of my regard for you and the joy I share
with you on this miraculous event.

Very sincerely,

_____

_____

Death in Agent's Family

[*Date*]

_____

_____

_____

Dear _____ :

Please accept my sincere condolences to you [*and your son*] on your recent loss. I know how much you thought of [*Mary Jane*] and can understand your feelings at this time.

[*Mary Jane*] brought joy to the lives of [*her*] family and friends, and [*her*] memory will live on in those whose lives [*she*] influenced.

[*According to your wishes, I have made a donation to (The American Cancer Society) in (Mary Jane's) name.*]

Thinking of you,

_____

_____

NOTE: *This personal note is sent in addition to any flowers you may have sent for the funeral.*

Death of Salesperson or Associate

[*Date*]

_____

_____

_____

Dear _____ :

I wish to offer my personal condolences to you. [*Mary*] was [*an associate broker / salesperson*] with [*Clyde Realty*] for [*seven years / all too short a time*]. [*She*] was liked and respected by all of us as well as by the many clients whose real estate needs [*she*] helped to meet. [*Mary*] gave unsparingly of [*herself*] in helping others.

I share in your feeling of loss and want you to know that [*Mary*] will be truly missed.

[*According to your wishes, I have made a donation to (The American Cancer Society) in (Mary's) name.*]

Yours truly,

_____

NOTE: *This letter would be sent to a spouse or parent upon the death of an agent.*

Agent Who Voluntarily Left Office

[*Date*]

_____

_____

_____

Dear _____ :

I would like to take this opportunity to thank you for your professional efforts with [*Clyde Realty*] over the past [*five years*].

I wish you [*happiness / success*] for your future [*however, I want you to know that you will always have a home with (Clyde Realty)*].

[*Of course, you will promptly receive all commissions upon closing of transactions, in accord with our agreement.*]

[*We would appreciate if you would return (office keys, signs, and so on) to us as soon as practical.*]

[*If in the future you need a recommendation, do not hesitate to contact me.*]

Sincerely,

_____

_____

NOTE: *This letter will help to keep your relationship open with an employee who may have left for perceived "greener pastures." It will aid in future agent cooperation if the agent joins a competing firm, and it will leave the door open for a possible return.*

Letter of Recommendation

[Date]

_____

_____

_____

[Dear _____ *: | To Whom It May Concern* _____ *:]*

[Janet Jones] worked for *[Clyde Realty]* from *[August 1988]* to *[June 1994]* as a *[real estate sales associate | REALTOR-Associate ®]*. *[Janet]* always exhibited the utmost integrity and a sincere desire to help others in meeting their housing needs. *[I would hire Janet Jones again without hesitation.]*

Yours truly,

_____

Notice to Salesperson—Termination

[*Date*]

_____

_____

_____

Dear _____ :

I am very sorry to inform you that we are unable to retain your services as a [*sales associate / REALTOR-Associate ®*] with [*Clyde Realty*]. [*I have enclosed your real estate license.*] [*Your contract rights for sales and listings in progress will be strictly honored by our office.*] [*I would appreciate if you would send me your office keys and return all (signs and lockboxes).*]

I wish you every success in your future endeavors, and if I can be of any help to you or if you have any questions, please contact me personally.

Sincerely,

_____

_____

NOTE: *Normally, you should handle this in a face-to-face meeting. Avoid criticism or any accusations of dishonesty, since either could be construed as libel.*

Chapter

14

Lender, Attorney and Settlement Letters

Request for Loan Requirements and Terms— General

[*Date*]

_____

_____

_____

Dear _____ :

Please supply me with your current prequalifying requirements and terms for presently available fixed-rate and adjustable-rate mortgages.

I would also appreciate receiving borrower prequalifying forms as well as several loan application packages.

Yours truly,

_____

_____

Request for Loan Terms—Specific Buyer

[*Date*]

_____

_____

_____

Dear _____ :

Please supply me with your current loan terms for a [*30-year, fixed-rate mortgage / 25-year, adjustable-rate mortgage / for a home in Middlebury Heights*]. The purchase price is [*$130,000*], and the buyer has a [*$30,000*] down payment.

I would appreciate if you would also include several loan applications.

Yours truly,

_____

cc: [*Buyer*]

Loan Application Transmittal

[*Date*]

_____

_____

_____

Dear _____ :

Enclosed you will find the completed loan application of [*John and Mary Brown*] for the purchase of a home located at [*65 Jupiter Lane*].

If you have any problems whatsoever or desire any additional information, please contact [*Meg Smith*] or me.

Yours truly,

_____

Enclosure: [*Loan application*]

cc: [*John and Mary Brown*]

_____

NOTE: *We suggest sending loan package by registered mail or private carrier where a record of receipt is available.*

Request to Lender To Expedite Loan Request

[*Date*]

_____

_____

_____

Dear _____ :

[*Mr. and Mrs. Smith*] recently applied for a loan through your office for the purchase of the home at [*111 Stardust Circle*].

Because of unusual needs of the [*seller / buyer*], it is necessary that this sale be closed by [*August 1, 1994*]. Although I realize that this places a strain on your office, I would nevertheless greatly appreciate any efforts you can provide to expedite this transaction.

Yours truly,

_____

cc: [Insert names of buyer and/or seller.]

_____

NOTE: *When time is important, regular calls should be made to check on the status of the loan.*

To Lender—Low Appraisal

[Date]

_____

_____

_____

RE: Appraisal for [give address]

Dear _____ :

I was surprised by the appraisal made on *[April 3]* for the property at *[1121 Hummingbird Circle]*, for *[Mr. and Mrs. Jones's]* loan application.

The appraisal of *[$60,750]* does not reflect recent sales in the area. I have enclosed a comparative market analysis based on all the sales in *[Orchard Ridge Subdivision]* within the past *[90 days]*. You will see from comparable sales that your appraisal as stated appears to be at least *[$40,000]* under current market value.

I would appreciate if the appraisal could be reviewed.

I have enjoyed our mutually beneficial relationship in the past, and hope to continue working with you in the future to arrange the financing for our real estate purchasers.

Yours truly,

_____

Enclosure: *[Comparative market analysis]*

Request for Abstract Update

[*Date*]

_____

_____

_____

Dear _____ :

Please update the enclosed abstract for the following described property: [insert legal description of property].

Please bill [*the seller, Thomas Pike*] for this service.

Yours truly,

_____

Enclosure: [*Abstract*]

cc: [Use names of buyer and/or seller.]

_____

NOTE: *The abstract should normally be delivered personally. If it is mailed or sent by messenger, obtain a receipt as proof of its delivery.*

Thank-You to Loan Officer #1

[*Date*]

_____

_____

_____

Dear _____ :

I would like to personally thank you for your help in arranging the financing for [*Sherman and Joyce Mack*] for their recent purchase of the home at [*72 Lynn Court*].

You not only delivered the loan in a timely manner, but you provided counseling service as well, which was greatly appreciated. You turned what is usually a difficult process for a buyer into a pleasant experience. I hope to work with you and your firm on many future loans.

Yours truly,

_____

Enclosure: [*Card*]

cc: [*Jane Smith, President, ABO Savings and Loan*]

NOTE: *A letter such as this, with copies sent to the president of the lending bank, S & L, or loan company, will be appreciated by the loan officer. You can expect this loan officer to treat any future loan problems as a priority item.*

Thank-You to Loan Officer #2

[*Date*]

_____

_____

_____

Dear _____ :

I want to thank you personally for your Herculean efforts that resulted in our closing the [*James C. Smith*] loan by [*August 1*].

Your attention to detail and your honest, straightforward approach proved that what others said couldn't be done *can* be accomplished with a positive, "can do" attitude. Working with you was a pleasure, and I look forward to many further transactions with your firm.

Yours truly,

_____

Enclosure: [*Card*]

cc: [*John Jones, President, ABC Savings and Loan*]

NOTE: *This letter and its copy will give you a future ally in the lender's office.*

Request for Loan Payoff Balance

[*Date*]

_____

_____

_____

Dear _____ :

Please provide the payoff balance for loan no. [*00190356,
23 Hummingbird Circle*] in the name of [*Janet Smith*], based on a
payoff date of [*January 1, 1996*].

Yours truly,

_____

cc: [*Janet Smith*]

Request for List of REOs

[*Date*]

_____

_____

_____

Dear _____ :

Please provide a list of your present repossessions and give the following information:

1. Address and size

2. Price and terms (if applicable)

3. Obtaining keys for showings (Is a master key available?)

Yours truly,

_____

Enclosure: [*Card*]

NOTE: *REO is the trade acronym for* real estate owned *by the lender that is acquired through foreclosure.*

Request for Attorney Title Opinion

[*Date*]

_____

_____

_____

Dear _____ :

Please provide a title opinion for [*Mr. and Mrs. Thomas Wooley*] for the purchase of [*insert legal descriptions of property*].

The updated abstract is enclosed.

Please send the opinion and the abstract to [*my office*]. Your invoice should be made out to [*Mr. and Mrs. Thomas Wooley, but sent to me*].

Yours truly,

_____

Enclosure: [*Abstract*]

cc: [*Mr. and Mrs. Thomas Wooley*]

NOTE: *Generally, abstracts should be hand-delivered to the attorney's office and a receipt should be obtained.*

Purchase Contract for [*Buyer's* / *Seller's*] Attorney Approval

[*Date*]

_____

_____

_____

Dear _____ :

Enclosed is the completed purchase contract for the [*sale by* / *purchase by*], [*Jim and Jane Schmidt*] of [*111 Crescent Cove*]. If after your review you determine that the agreement is legally sufficient, please have [*Mr. and Mrs. Schmidt*] sign and return [*three*] copies to this office.

Yours truly,

_____

Enclosure: [*Purchase contract*]

cc: [*Jim and Jane Schmidt*]

NOTE: *Don't mention changes or modifications. Most attorneys will do so without your reminder.*

Thank-You Letter to Attorney

[*Date*]

_____

_____

_____

Dear _____ :

Working with you on the [*Smiths'*] [*sale / purchase*] was a pleasure. Your professional and helpful manner made what is often a confrontation a friendly and beneficial transaction.

If I am ever asked to recommend a real estate attorney, I will not hesitate to provide your name.

Yours truly,

_____

Enclosure: [*Card*]

NOTE: *A thank-you letter such as this will help you to deal with the attorney in a more relaxed manner in the future.*

Request for Escrow Fee and Cost Schedules

[*Date*]

_____

_____

_____

Dear _____ :

Please supply me with your current escrow fee schedule as well as
your schedule of escrow costs.

Yours truly,

_____

Request for Private Mortgage Insurance Information

[*Date*]

_____

_____

_____

Dear _____ :

Please send me information on your requirements for and costs of private mortgage insurance. Please also include several application packages.

Yours truly,

_____

Inquiry about Home Protection Warranty

[*Date*]

_____

_____

_____

Dear _____ :

Please send me information, costs and coverage for your home warranty programs as well as several application packages.

Yours truly,

_____

Inquiry about Escrow Status for Closing

[*Date*]

_____

_____

_____

Dear _____ :

Please provide me with the present status of the escrow for closing on [*111 West Jackson Street*], [*Hirt—sellers and Scallon—buyers*].

If there is any problem that could prevent a [*June 1*] closing, please contact me at once. Thank you.

Yours truly,

_____

Enclosure: [*Card*]

cc: [*J. Hirt and L. Scallon*]

Release of Earnest Money

[*Date*]

_____

_____

_____

Dear _____ :

Your [*sale / purchase*] of the property at [_____]
cannot be completed because [_____].

[*Please sign and return the enclosed authorization to return the
earnest money deposit to the buyers, (Mr. and Mrs. Tom Jones).*]

[*Please sign and return the enclosed release authorizing that your
earnest money deposit be turned over to the owners, (Mr. and Mrs.
Henry Smith), as liquidated damages in accord with your purchase
agreement. This will relieve you of all further obligations under the
purchase contract.*]

Yours truly,

_____

Enclosure: [*Release of deposit*]

cc: [*Mr. and Mrs. Tom Jones / Mr. and Mrs. Henry Smith*]

NOTE: *If a standard release form is not used, have your attorney
prepare an appropriate release form.*

Order To Return or Turn Over Deposit

[*Date*]

_____

_____

_____

To: [*Escrow agent / Attorney holding a deposit*]

Dear _____ :

You are holding an earnest money deposit for [$ _____], pursuant to a [*purchase agreement*] dated [_____], in which [*buyers*] agreed to buy [give address and description of property] from [*sellers*]. [*Enclosed is a release authorization signed by (buyers / sellers).*]

You are hereby authorized to [*return / turn over*] [*the deposit / the sum of $* _____] to [*buyers / sellers*].

Yours truly,

_____

cc: [Give names of buyers/sellers.]

NOTE: *This is an order to a third-party escrow holder about return of deposit money when the sale will not be completed. The sellers must agree to the return of the deposit to the buyers, and the buyers must agree to turn over their deposit to the seller.*

Chapter

15

Press Releases

Always obtain the buyer's and/or the seller's permission before sending out a press release about a buyer, a seller or a sale.

Transmittal Letter—Press Release

[*Date*]

_____

_____

_____

Dear _____ :

Enclosed is a press release [*as well as a photograph with caption*] concerning [*Mr. Frederick Schmidt, who has recently been awarded the Certified Residential Specialist designation.*]

[*We believe this is a significant achievement that deserves community recognition.*]

If you have any questions or desire further information, please contact me.

Yours truly,

_____

_____

Enclosure: [*Photo and Press release*]

NOTE: *Use masking tape as a hinge on the back of the photo so that the caption can be read below the high-contrast, black and white, glossy 5 × 7.*

New Owner

[*Retired Banker Chooses Meadowbrook*]

Mr. and Mrs. [*Angus McCook*] have recently purchased [*a new home on Clancy Lane in Meadowbrook*]. [*Mr. McCook was active in banking for 40 years, having started as a teller with the Midvale Bank and rising to the presidency of the Newport Banking Group, one of the largest bank holding companies in the state.*]

[*Mr. and Mrs. McCook*] indicated that they were attracted to Meadowbrook because of [*the choice of several outstanding golf courses, its general country atmosphere, and its proximity to the amenities of urban life*]. The purchase was arranged through the [*Meadowbrook office of Clyde Realty*].

Enclosure: Photo

NOTE: *A press release about a buyer is appropriate when the buyer has a distinguished or interesting background. Photos with captions should be included.*

Always obtain the buyer's permission before publicizing a purchase.

Sale and Purchase

[*Smith Building (Sold)*]

[*Jim Anderson*] of [*Clyde Realty*] recently sold [*the Smith Building*] at [*5 Commercial Avenue*]. The former owners, [*Alice and Gertrude Smith*], owned this landmark property for [*45*] years.

The purchasers, [*Mr. and Mrs. Thomas Blake*] of [*San Juno*], have indicated that they will [*extensively remodel the property / move their offices to the property*]. [*Mr. Blake is president of Blake Motors in Covina.*]

[*This sale brings the first quarter sales of Clyde Realty to over $17 million, which is an increase of 16 percent from last year's sales. Mr. Joseph Clyde, vice president of sales, has indicated that interest in large commercial properties such as the Smith Building has increased significantly, and he predicts continued sales increases in the foreseeable future.*]

Enclosure: Photo

NOTE: *If a building is well known or has historical significance, a press release would be appropriate when it is listed for sale or sold.*

Include a captioned photo of the property, possibly with the buyers and the agent in front of the property.

Always obtain permission of both buyer and seller to publicize a sale.

Groundbreaking

New Project—[*Woodlake Village*]

[*Wilson Developers*] held their official groundbreaking for the new, [*122 single-family home Woodlake Village development*] on [*Wednesday, March 1*]. Located [*on the northwest corner of Dunn Road and Woodlake Parkway*], the [*three- and four-bedroom family homes*] will feature [*up to 2,400 square feet. All homes will have three-car garages, tile roofs and Eurostyle kitchens*].

[*Peggy Wilson*], project sales coordinator for [*Clyde Realty*] and the exclusive sales agent for [*Woodlake Village*], has indicated that the choice location coupled with moderate prices, starting at [*$122,500*] with [*seven percent*] financing, has already created an exceptional word-of-mouth interest in the development. According to [*Peggy Wilson*], the early reservations have been primarily from professionals in the real estate and construction industries.

Enclosure: Photo

NOTE: *For groundbreaking ceremonies, consider including a captioned photograph with local civic leaders and a builder representative as well as an agent of your firm. A captioned artist's rendering of a model home would also be appropriate.*

Subdivision Opening

Grand Opening—[*Woodlake Village*]

The grand opening of [*Wilson Development's*] new [*Wood-lake Village*] is scheduled for [*Saturday and Sunday, June 5th and 6th*]. Located [*on the northwest corner of Dunn Road and Woodlake Parkway*], the development features [*three- and four-bedroom family homes starting at $122,500, with 7¼ percent financing available*]. All homes include [*three-car garages, tile roofs, and Eurostyle kitchens*].

[*Peggy Wilson*], the [*sales coordinator*] for [*Clyde Realty*], which is the exclusive sales agent for the project, has indicated that exceptional interest has developed in [*Woodlake Village*] due to [its *choice location and the moderate pricing policy*].

According to [*Mrs. Wilson*], [*the grand opening will feature six decorator-furnished models, and there will be refreshments and gifts for opening-day visitors*].

Enclosure: Photo

NOTE: *You should include a photo or artist's rendering of one of the models. Placing ads on the opening generally ensures publication of your press release.*

First Sale in Subdivision

First Sale Made at [*English Village*]

[*Clyde Realty*], the exclusive sales agent for [*English Village*], has announced that [*Dr. and Mrs. Timothy Marks*] are the first home purchasers in [*the exclusive enclave of 16 estate homes in Bellwood*]. [*Dr. Marks is a pediatrician and is on the staff of Mercy Hospital.*]

The [*Marks*] chose a [*3,600 square-foot English country design*]. According to [*Dr. Marks*], they decided on [*English Village*] because of [*the huge lots, scenic views, quality design and construction as well as the country ambience, which is so important with four small children*].

[*Currently, three of the estate homes are under construction with the Marks's home scheduled for completion by August 15.*]

Enclosure: Photo

NOTE: *For a press release that provides information about a buyer, be certain to obtain permission from the buyer. A captioned picture of the purchasing family standing in front of the home, even if the home is not completed, would be appropriate.*

In addition to publicity about your firm, a press release such as this one significantly reduces the possibility that the buyer will attempt to avoid the purchase closing.

Milestone Sale in Subdivision

[*100th Sale Announced for Orchard Heights*]

[*Henry Ammenson*], [*project director*] for [*Clyde Realty*], has announced that the [*100th new home in Orchard Heights has been sold since November*]. According to [*Mr. Ammenson*], this subdivision has been one of the most successful in the area because of the tremendous value offered in housing at a premier location. The problem has been not being able to build the homes fast enough. [*Mr. Ammenson indicates that, at the present sales rate, the entire subdivision will be sold out by June 1.*]

Enclosure: Photo

NOTE: *Consider a captioned photograph of the buying family in front of their new home. Never send a press release out about a transaction, buyer, or seller without written permission from the people involved.*

Office Opening or Relocation

[Clyde Realty Opens Newhall Office /
Clyde Realty Expands]

[*Clyde Realty*] has announced [*the opening of a (second) office (in the Murray Building at 136 West 31st Street in Lynnwood). / the relocation of its Lynnwood office to the Murray Building at 136 West 31st Street.*]

According to [*Thomas Johnson, President of Clyde Realty*], the [*expansion / move*] was necessary to better meet the needs of [*Lynnwood*] residents.

Although the office will specialize in [*residential sales*], its services will also include [*investment sales and property management*]. [*The new office will also coordinate the sales of several new subdivisions in the area.*] [*Clyde Realty*] currently has [*more than 60 salespeople with total sales last year exceeding $100 million, making the firm one of the fastest-growing brokerage offices in the county!*]

Enclosure: Photo

NOTE: *Consider a captioned photograph of the entire office staff in front of the new office or with a "For Sale" sign.*

New Associate or Salesperson

[*Henry Gibbs*] joins [*Clyde Realty*]

[*Thomas Flynn*], [*General Manager*] of [*Clyde Realty*], announced that [*Mr. Henry Gibbs*] recently joined the firm as a [*sales associate / REALTOR-Associate ® / associate broker*]. [*Mr. Gibbs*] will be involved with [*home sales, primarily in the West Valley*].

[*Mr. Gibbs*] is [*a graduate of Syracuse University and has spent 12 years as a food broker in Chicago*]. [*He*] obtained [*his*] real estate license [*two years ago, and he was previously associated with Boniface Construction Company, selling new homes in the Bellwood Heights development*]. [*Mr. Gibbs is a member of Thunderbird Country Club and resides in Bellwood Heights with his wife Eileen and their two daughters.*]

Enclosure: Photo

NOTE: Send a captioned photo with all personnel press releases.

Promotion or Appointment

New [*Sales Manager*]

[*Henry Clyde, President of Clyde Realty*] has announced that [*Janet Jones*] has been appointed [*sales manager*] of [*Clyde Realty*].

[*Ms. Jones*] brings a wealth of experience to the position. [*She*] was formerly associated with [*Smith Realty*] as [*assistant sales manager*]. [*Ms. Jones*] has had over [*eight*] years of experience in [*sales / real estate sales*]. [*Ms. Jones*] has been with [*Clyde Realty*] for [*four years*]. [*Ms. Jones has received numerous honors, including membership in the prestigious Clyde Realty Million Dollar Roundtable.*]

[*Ms. Jones received her bachelor's degree in business from Yale University. / Ms. Jones attended New York University.*] [*She*] lives with [*her*] family in [*Midvale Heights*]. [*She has two children, John, nine years old, and Tammy, six.*] [*Her husband Clarence teaches English at South High School*]. [*Ms. Jones*] is active in [*Soroptimists and is an assistant Girl Scout leader*].

Enclosure: Photo

NOTE: *Consider a captioned photo of a broker with the new* [sales manager] *either in front of the office or near an office sign. If the person did not graduate from a school, you can use "attended." If she or he graduated, indicate "graduated from" or the degree received.*

Professional Designation

[*Jim Jones Earns Professional Designation*]

[*Jim Jones*], a [*n*] [*sales associate / associate broker / REALTOR-Associate ®*] with [*Clyde Realty*], has recently earned the coveted [*Certified Residential Specialist (CRS)*] designation. This [*is the highest*] professional award of the [*Residential Sales Council*] and is awarded only after a [*REALTOR ® / real estate professional*] has met [*high standards for experience and has also completed a rigorous course of training*]. [*Mr. Jones*] is now one of just a few real estate professionals in [*our community*] who may use [*CRS*] after [*his / her*] name.

[*Mr. Jones has been a real estate professional for 17 years. He is a graduate of Notre Dame where he earned his degree in marketing. He lives in Westwood with his wife, Ellen, and their two daughters. Mr. Jones is active in the Rotary Club and is a deacon at Westwood Community Church.*]

Enclosure: Photo

Sales Award

Salesperson of the [*Month* / *Year*]

[*Joseph Evans*], [*Sales Manager*] of [*Clyde Realty*], has announced that [*Patricia Jones*] has been named [*sales associate*] of the [*month* / *year*].

During [*March* / *the past year*], [*Ms. Jones*] has [*sold* / *listed*] [*more than $3 million in real estate* / *19 properties*]. [*Ms. Jones*] has been associated with [*Clyde Realty*] [*since 1983* / *for seven years*]. Before joining [*Clyde Realty*], [*she*] was [*a professor of zoology at Western State University*]. [*Ms. Jones lives in Middletown with her husband and four children.*]

Enclosure: Photo

NOTE: *Enclose a photo of a broker and the salesperson receiving an award.*

Sale of Real Estate Firm

New Owner Announced for [*Clyde Realty*]

[*Clyde Realty*] has announced that the firm has been sold [*by its founder, Angus Clyde, to the firm's General Manager, Thomas Flynn. Angus Clyde founded Clyde Realty in 1947, and it has been the oldest real estate firm in the county under the same ownership*].

[*Clyde Realty*] currently has [*62 salespeople operating from their offices at 922 West Broadway*]. [*Angus Clyde*] estimates that since it was founded, the firm has sold over [*25,000*] properties, with total sales [*in the hundreds of millions of dollars*].

[*Thomas Flynn has been associated with Clyde Realty for 11 years, starting as a salesperson, and has served the last four years as General Manager. Mr. Flynn, who is a business graduate of Michigan State University, indicates that the firm's name, as well as the philosophy and policies of Angus Clyde, will continue.*]

Enclosure: Photo

NOTE: *Include a photograph showing both former owner (if possible) and successor.*

Chapter

16

Miscellaneous Letters

Letter to Newspaper about Ad Copy—
Transmittal

[*Date*]

_____

_____

_____

Dear _____ :

I wish to run the following ads [*from Sunday, April 3 through Saturday, April 9 / on Sunday, April 3*] in the classified section under the following categories:

Category: _____

_____

_____

_____

_____

Category: _____

_____

_____

_____

_____

Please bill these ads to our account.

Yours Truly,

⎡ *Thomas Flynn* ⎤
⎣ *Clyde Realty* ⎦

NOTE: *Give any instructions about size or style of type, if applicable.*

Notice to Newspaper of Mistake
in Advertisement

[*Date*]

_____

_____

_____

Attention: Classified Advertisement Department Editor

Dear [*Editor / To Whom it May Concern*]:

On [*September 10*] we placed an ad under the category [*Real Estate*] to run on [*Sunday, September 16*].

The ad was to read as follows: _____

_____

_____

Due to your error, the ad appeared on [give date(*s*)] on page [*37*], [*under the category (Appliances), [and read as follows*]: _____

_____

_____

Because of the error, [*the effectiveness of the ad was materially diminished / the ad was of no benefit to our firm*]. We therefore expect [*an appropriate adjustment because of your error / the ad charge to be fully credited on our next billing / the ad to be reproduced as placed on (give date(s)) without charge*].

Yours truly,

_____

_____

Charity Ticket Response

[*Date*]

_____

_____

_____

Dear _____ :

Enclosed is our check for [*$30*] for [*two*] tickets. The remaining tickets are enclosed.

We are always happy to provide assistance to local organizations. We wish you good luck on your event.

Yours truly,

_____

_____

NOTE: *Charities generally send out books of tickets. This response allows you to be positive without having to buy all of the tickets.*

Christmas Card Caption

May the joyous holiday spirit
extend throughout the coming year.
Wishing you and yours a very special

Season's Greetings

from all of us at
[*Clyde Realty*]*!*

NOTE: *This short season's greetings would be appropriate with a photograph of your staff and families or with the personal signatures of your staff.*

Holiday Open House Invitation

[*Clyde Realty*]

Cordially Invites You to Our

Holiday Season Open House

[*922 West 52nd Street*]

[*Friday December 23rd*]

[*5–7 PM*]

Please Visit with Us

[*922 West 52nd Street*]

Refreshments will be served.

(Sprig of holly here)

NOTE: *Invitations should be on regular invitation card stock. Send to other brokers, lenders, investors, owners, and so on.*

Thank You for Referring Your Friend

[*Date*]

_____

_____

_____

Dear _____ :

I want to thank you for referring your friend [*John Jones*] to our office.

Referrals such as yours let us know that we are doing a good job of meeting the real estate needs of our neighbors.

I [*am working with Mr. and Mrs. Jones to find them a new home / was successful in finding a lovely new home for Mr. and Mrs. Jones / was able to find a buyer for the Jones's lovely home / feel certain I will be able to find a buyer for the Jones's lovely home*].

I want you to know that we will appreciate any future referrals, and I will strive to meet the needs of your friends.

Very sincerely,

_____

_____

_____

INDEX

New

CD-ROM Money Maker Kits from Dearborn Multimedia

Book & CD-ROM Set

A DEARBORN MONEY MAKER KIT

THE MORTGAGE KIT

THIRD EDITION

SELECT THE RIGHT LOAN
NEGOTIATE THE BEST TERMS
LOCK IN THE LOWEST RATE
UNDERSTAND ALL YOUR OPTIONS

THOMAS C. STEINMETZ
PHILLIP WHITT

Features:

- *25 minute video help with the author*
- *12-28 interactive printable forms per CD-ROM*
- *On-Line glossary of terms*
- *Quick-start video tutorial*
- *Interactive printable book on CD-ROM*
  (Print out sections you like for closer reading or writing notes.)

Start Enjoying Greater Financial Freedom
Triple Your Investment Portfolio

SAVE Thousands on Real Estate as a Buyer or Seller

Successfully Start & Manage a **NEW** Business

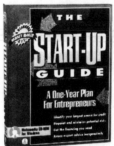

HOW TO INSTALL AND USE THE SOFTWARE

To Install the Application

For Windows

- Insert the disk in drive A: (or B:).
- From Program Manager or the Start menu select **Run.**
- Enter A:\Setup.exe.
- Follow prompts on screen.

How To Use This Application

The forms processing application provides a minimized word processor to allow you to customize, revise, and change the forms and letters contained on this disk. We've provided it to allow you to be productive immediately with the forms and/or letters contained in this guide. To open the application from Program Manager or the Start menu, select the Dearborn program group and click on the icon. The basic commands and features of the application are described below.

To Select a Form To Edit

Select the **File** and **Open Form** command to access the forms available with this application. The Open Form command presents the forms dialog box where you can select a form to customize. To select a form, click on a title in the list on the left side of the dialog box. The form title and a brief description of the form appear on the right side of the dialog box. If this is the form you want to edit, select **Open.**

Editing the Form

To edit the form and customize it for your use, select the **Find** button in the toolbar at the top of the form window to automatically locate fields in the form where you need to enter information. These fields are noted with a ">". Of course, you may change or revise any of the text in the form at will.

The menu at the top of the form provides you with several controls. These are as follows:

- **Edit**: You can cut, copy, and paste segments of text.
- **Style**: you can bold, italicize, and underline text, as well as select a font and type size for selected text.

Many of the functions available as menu selections are also available as button commands in the toolbar. These are:

- **Font:** Select from the fonts available on your system by pressing the down arrow and clicking on the font name.
- **Size:** Select the font size by clicking the down arrow and highlighting the font size.
- **Bold (B), Italic (I), Underline (U):** Select the text you want to change and press the button to change the format.
- **Justification:** You may change the text to flush right, left, centered, or justified by selecting the text and pressing the appropriate button.

Note: Save any edited forms under a different or new file name.

Favorites

If you are like most people, you'll likely use a few forms repeatedly. This application allows you to save forms as "favorites" to provide quick access to those forms frequently used. **To add a form to Favorites:**

- Open a form as you normally would.

- Choose **Favorites** from the File menu and select **Add to Favorites.**

- Enter the name for the file and choose Save. (The file will be saved in a default directory called RE_FAVS.)

- To reselect the form, select Favorites from the menu, and select Open Favorite Files. Select the file and press Open.

Help

To learn more about the forms application and the commands available to you, select **Help** from the menu.

If You Already Have a Word Processor . . .

If you have and are already familiar with one or more of the word processing applications available to you, you can use the functionality available in those programs to work with these forms. Select and edit any one of the forms directly from the forms subdirectory created on your hard drive during installation. The files are unformatted ASCII text files that work with all current applications. Text that you need to enter in order to complete a form is preceded by a ">" character. Using your word processor's search function to locate these areas will allow you to quickly customize the forms/letters to suit your needs.

Another way to use the forms in this application with other word processors is to save the file as either a text file (txt) or rich text file (rtf). To do this, select **File** and **Open** from the menu. Open the file you wish to edit and choose **Save As.** Select or enter the name of the file and choose the location where you want it to go. Select **OK.** Open the file in your word processor as you would any other file and edit. (Keep in mind that once you work on a file in another word processor and save it, it probably won't work in the forms processor application without conversion back to a standard text or ASCII file .)

TECHNICAL SUPPORT IS NOT AVAILABLE ON THE ENCLOSED COMPUTER DISK. Please read the installation and operating instructions carefully before attempting to use the disk.

LICENSE AGREEMENT

OPENING ENVELOPE VOIDS RETURNABILITY OR MONEY-BACK GUARANTEES
PLEASE READ THIS DOCUMENT CAREFULLY BEFORE BREAKING THIS SEAL

By breaking this sealed envelope, you agree to become bound by the terms of this license. If you do not agree to the terms of this license do not use the software and promptly return the unopened package within thirty (30) days to the place where you obtained it for a refund.

This Software is licensed, not sold to you by DEARBORN FINANCIAL PUBLISHING, INC. owner of the product for use only under the terms of this License, and DEARBORN FINANCIAL PUBLISHING, INC. reserves any rights not expressly granted to you.

1. **LICENSE**: This License allows you to:

(a) Use the Software only on a single microcomputer at a time, except the Software may be executed from a common disk shared by multiple CPU's provided that one authorized copy of the Software has been licensed from DEARBORN FINANCIAL PUBLISHING, INC. for each CPU executing the Software. DEARBORN FINANCIAL PUBLISHING, INC. does not, however, guarantee that the Software will function properly in your multiple CPU, multi-user environment. The Software may not be used with any gateways, bridges, modems, and/or network extenders that allow the software to be used on multiple CPU's unless one authorized copy of the Software has been licensed from DEARBORN FINANCIAL PUBLISHING, INC. for each CPU executing the Software.

(b) The Software can be loaded to the harddrive and the disk kept solely for backup purposes. The Software is protected by United States copyright law. You must reproduce on each copy the copyright notice and any other proprietary legends that were on the original copy supplied by DEARBORN FINANCIAL PUBLISHING, INC.

(c) Configure the Software for your own use by adding or removing fonts, desk accessories, and/or device drivers.

2. **RESTRICTION:** You may not distribute copies of the Software to others or electronically transfer the Software from one computer to another over a network and/or zone. The Software contains trade secrets and to protect them you may not de-compile, reverse engineer, disassemble, cross assemble or otherwise change and/or reduce the Software to any other form. You may not modify, adapt, translate, rent, lease, loan, resell for profit, distribute, network, or create derivative works based upon the Software or any part thereof.

3. **TERMINATION:** This License is effective unless terminated. This License will terminate immediately without notice from DEARBORN FINANCIAL PUBLISHING, INC. if you fail to comply with any provision of this License. Upon termination you must destroy the Software and all copies thereof. You may terminate the License at any time by destroying the Software and all copies thereof.

4. **EXPORT LAW ASSURANCES:** You agree that the Software will not be shipped, transferred or exported into any country prohibited by the United States Export Administration Act and the regulations thereunder nor will be used for any purpose prohibited by the Act.

5. **LIMITED WARRANTY, DISCLAIMER, LIMITATION OF REMEDIES AND DAMAGES:** The information in this software (Materials) is sold with the understanding that the author, publisher, developer and distributor are not engaged in rendering legal, accounting, banking, security or other professional advice. If legal advice, accounting advice, security investment advice, bank or tax advice or other expert professional assistance is required, the services of a competent professional with expertise in that field should be sought. These materials have been developed using ideas from experience and survey information from various research, lectures and publications. The information contained in these materials is believed to be reliable only at the time of publication and it cannot be guaranteed as it is applied to any particular individual or situation. The author, publisher, developer and distributor specifically disclaim any liability, or risk, personal or otherwise, incurred directly or indirectly as a consequence of the use an application of the information contained in these materials or the live lectures that could accompany their distribution. In no event will the author, publisher, developer or distributor be liable to the purchaser for any amount greater that the purchase price of these materials.

DEARBORN FINANCIAL PUBLISHING, INC.'S warranty on the media, including any implied warranty of merchant ability or fitness for a particular purpose, is limited in duration to thirty (30) days from the date of the original retail. If a disk fails to work or if a disk becomes damaged, you may obtain a replacement disk by returning the original disk and a check or money order for $5.00, for each replacement disk, together with a brief explanation note and a dated sales receipt to:

DEARBORN FINANCIAL PUBLISHING, INC.
155 NORTH WACKER DRIVE
CHICAGO, IL 60606-1719

The replacement warranty set forth above is the sole and exclusive remedy against DEARBORN FINANCIAL PUBLISHING, INC. for breach of warrant, express or implied or for any default whatsoever relating to condition of the software. DEARBORN FINANCIAL PUBLISHING, INC. makes no other warranties or representation, either expressed or implied, with respect to this software or documentation, quality, merchantability performance or fitness for a particular purpose as a result. This software is sold with only the limited warranty with respect to diskette replacement as provided above, and you, the Licensee, are assuming all other risks as to its quality and performance. In no event will DEARBORN FINANCIAL PUBLISHING, INC. or its developers, directors, officers, employees, or affiliates be liable for direct , incidental, indirect, special or consequential damages (including damages for loss of business profits, business interruption, loss of business information and the like) resulting from any defect in this software or its documentation or arising out of the use of or inability to use the software or accompanying documentation even if DEARBORN FINANCIAL PUBLISHING, INC. an authorized DEARBORN FINANCIAL PUBLISHING, INC. representative, or a DEARBORN FINANCIAL PUBLISHING, INC. affiliate has been advised of the possibility of such damage.

DEARBORN FINANCIAL PUBLISHING, INC. MAKES NO REPRESENTATION OR WARRANTY REGARDING THE RESULTS OBTAINABLE THROUGH USE OF THE SOFTWARE.

No oral or written information or advice given by DEARBORN FINANCIAL PUBLISHING, INC. its dealers, distributors, agents, affiliates, developers, officers, directors, or employees shall create a warranty or in any way increase the scope of this warranty.

Some states do not allow the exclusion or limitation of implied warranties or liabilities for incidental or consequential, damages, so the above limitation or exclusion may not apply to you. This warranty gives you specific legal rights, and you may also have other rights which vary from state to state.

COPYRIGHT NOTICE: This software and accompanying manual are copyrighted with all rights reserved by DEARBORN FINANCIAL PUBLISHING, INC. Under United States copyright laws, the software and its accompanying documentation may not be copied in whole or in part except in normal use of the software or the reproduction of a backup copy for archival purpose only. Any other copying, selling or otherwise distributing this software or manual is hereby expressly forbidden.

SIGNATURE_____

SIGN IF BEING RETURNED UNOPENED FOR REFUND